Sealed for a Purpose

a journey toward the final millennium

Phillip Moore

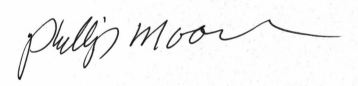
Xulon
PRESS

Dedication

To my loving wife, Patti.
Without her encouragement and perseverance this book could not
have been possible.

To my children, their families and my friends who were sounding
boards and who gave technical advice and logistical support.

To Ray Boltz whose music unlocked the chains of writer's block.

**Most of all I thank God that He has allowed me this
opportunity to be a witness for Him.**

INTRODUCTION

‡══‡

In the past Satan has attempted to destroy the line of kinship to the Redeemer. King Joash of Israel is the one who was the sole survivor of such an attempt. From age one he was hidden away from those who would kill him. When he was seven years old, he was made king. Had the attempts on his life been successful the genealogy to the Messiah would have been stopped. When Zedekiah was captured by Nebuchadnezzar all his male heirs were brought before him and killed. The king was led away into captivity where he died. The king's two daughters were taken to a place of safety by the prophet Jeremiah and the line of ancestry was preserved.

Soon after Jesus was born Herod ordered the death of all the babies in the area in an effort to kill the infant Jesus. Satan was once again prevented from succeeding in his attempt. Some time later Satan himself entered into Judas and in one last great attempt to kill the Redeemer, he was allowed by God the Father to succeed. Through Satan's efforts to destroy God's plan, he actually caused the plan of redemption to be made complete.

In *Sealed for a Purpose – a journey toward the final millennium,* an ordinary couple learn that they are part of an extraordinary genealogical line. Although spiritual warfare surrounds them, they are supernaturally protected by angelic forces. They have been sealed for a purpose.

This is their story.

CHAPTER 1

―==―

10:01 PM JUNE 12 INDIANAPOLIS, INDIANA

The soot stained brick of the old downtown office building muffled the sound of the distant rumblings of thunder. No one could have been less aware of the passing storm than the two employees working late night hours at the Hoosier Tribune. A lone reporter, lost in thought, put the finishing touches on his column. He meticulously checked his charts and graphs, making certain all figures were accurate. As a journalism major in college, he often dreamed of winning the Pulitzer Prize for his work. But that was 15 years earlier. These days he found satisfaction in doing simple jobs well.

Reporter Tom Alexander pushed himself back from his cluttered desk, put his arms over his head and stretched his lean six-foot frame. For an instant he wondered if the creaking noises he heard were coming from his ancient chair or his aching bones. Working late to meet deadlines was taking its toll. Even though he loved his job, work was work. He breathed out a long sigh. Tomorrow would be different. A short vacation was at hand.

As if reality had a volume control, Tom became increasingly aware of the sounds from the next office as Sam, the night custodian went about his usual perfectionist routine cleaning and rearranging things.

When Sam Keller pulled his hitch in the army, he soon learned that all things had to be perfectly aligned as if every day were a General Inspection Day. He walked to the back of the office, stood behind the last desk and bent over to look at the desks, neatly aligned in their row of six. Each desk lamp, computer monitor, pencil holder, and desk pad on all six desks were identically placed.

"Ahhh," Sam exhaled heartily as he smiled and mentally gave himself a pat on the back for a job well done. He finished his night shift job every day feeling good about the way he left the place. He wondered if the daytimers who worked at those desks even noticed his touch.

In the old days, people appreciated such things. Sam mused as he looked around the room, and remembered when the furnishings were new. He had come straight from the army at the end of World War II to work for the Hoosier Tribune when it was a bustling daily newspaper. He had made a career of this job. He felt like the place was his and was only slightly offended when computers invaded his turf. At times he still longed for the "pencil and paper" days, but he knew that computers had saved the business from failure as it changed from a daily to a weekly newspaper. The old ways of doing things couldn't save it but at least the computers' efficiency had kept the paper alive.

In the next room, Tom stood up and ran his fingers through his sandy hair. He absently noted his overdue haircut, another detail he hadn't taken care of. He extended his arms and rolled his shoulders in an attempt to work out the kinks. Once again he had sat in one position too long. A soft, weary yawn from Tom got Sam's attention.

"Hi there, Mr. Tom," Sam said as he entered the office to greet the sole holdover from the daylight hours. Sam used the term "Mr. Tom" as a combination of respect for Tom's position, yet indicating a friendly familiarity. He felt uncomfortable using Mr. Alexander, but even more uncomfortable calling Tom by his first name. "Mr. Tom" he decided was a practical compromise.

"Hey, Sam," was the reply from a voice still distorted from an ongoing stretch.

"I know you work over a lot, but this is really late. You workin' on anything special?" Sam asked, hoping to bait Tom into telling him why he was there at 10:00 P.M. The bait worked.

"Just wrapping up some loose ends so I can start vacation tomorrow. No more paperwork for at least a week. By the way, Sam, you can use my desk and parking space while I'm gone."

"Thanks, Mr. Tom. That parking space will save me lots of steps, and I can use your phone to call the wife while I eat my lunch."

"How is your wife and family, Sam?"

"The wife's doing fine, I guess. She's so busy with those women's groups and mission projects down at the church. That's all she talks about. You know how it is."

"Oh, I know all right," chuckled Tom.

Sam paused for a second and said thoughtfully, "You know my son Willie?"

"Yes. Is he making retirement soon?"

"He was all set to retire from the Air Force until about three months ago. Then he said that he would wait until he had twenty-five years in instead of twenty. He always said he wanted to retire before his old man did. Then, all of a sudden, he changed his mind. That retirement used to be a big joke between us, but now Willie seems to be real serious about his work."

"Did his job change?" Tom asked.

"I don't know for sure," replied Sam. "He never has talked much about that. But you know he works at the Pentagon. Now he's working on some General's staff."

"Oh, really?"

"Yeah, the boy's a Lieutenant Colonel now. The missus and I are proud of him. He's done good all through high school, college and ROTC."

"Well, Sam, don't worry about it. When some people get close to retirement, they get cold feet and simply want to keep on working."

"Oh, that's probably it," said Sam. "You gonna take all this camera stuff on vacation?"

"I'm trying to decide what to take."

"Sure hope you have better weather. Storms like we had tonight can really mess up a vacation."

"Storm…What storm?"

"Where you been, Mr. Tom? Inside that computer of yours?"

"I must have been."

Sam grinned. "Tell you the truth, Mr. Tom, I didn't know about it myself till I looked out the window and saw everything wet and lightning flashin' way over yonder."

"Oh, no."

"What?"

"My car, I just cleaned it up. Wait a minute. There was no storm in the forecast."

"Ain't that just the way it goes? Win some, lose some, a few get rained out!" chuckled Sam, pleased with his little joke.

Tom grinned as he started picking up his equipment.

"Can I help you carry any of that stuff, Mr. Tom?"

"No, thanks. I just wanted to take my cameras and some film home instead of leaving all this stuff here in the way. I'm having a tough time trying to decide which camera to take with us tomorrow. There's not much room. The car's not very big!"

The two men had talked their way to the front lobby door with Tom wearily carrying five leather cases with straps of cameras, film, and equipment slung over his right shoulder. Sam thought Tom looked like a Santa out of uniform.

Sam unlocked the glass door. Rivulets of water were running down the glass. The water drops increased in size and picked up speed as they collided with other drops on their fall to the doorsill. The little rivulets formed streams that ran off and disappeared into the semi-darkness and shadows from the parking lot lights.

Sam looked out into the lot at Tom's parking space. Each space had an employees name painted on it. Tom's space was near the walk close to the front lobby. Sam's space was quite a distance further. There were only two vehicles in the lot at this hour, Sam's old gray minivan and Tom's red 1957 Thunderbird.

Sam chuckled. "I see what you mean about the car being so little. You and the missus gonna spend a week in that car? You wanna borrow mine? I'll be glad to swap with you for a week…maybe longer."

The twinkle in Sam's eye projected the vision in his mind. The very thought of "toolin" around town in that candy apple red car with the big, wide white walls brought a smile to his weathered face… but then many smiles had found a home on Sam's face over the years. He was a happy man.

Tom just stared at the car. He didn't even respond to the offer to swap vehicles.

With a tight look on his face, Tom said, "You know, you spend four hours cleaning, buffing, waxing, polishing, and doing all the other things you do to baby a car you've loved for years. You bring it to work and let it sit in the parking lot all day. Then it rains before you can get it back home."

As Sam held the door opened, he laughed out loud at Tom's frustration at having to clean the car again.

"You'll clean it again, Mr. Tom, and love every minute of it."

"Yeah, you're right. I'll see you in a week, Sam."

"Have a good time, Mr. Tom."

As he turned toward his car, Tom heard the bolt click as Sam locked the door and started back to his work.

The rain had slowed to a fine mist. Tom noticed that the storm clouds had moved off to the northwest…northwest??? Tom was puzzled. "This storm pattern is odd," he muttered, "weather patterns move from west to east around here this time of year. Oh, well I don't make storms," he said dismissing the thought from his mind, as he walked toward the car.

Water beads on the T-bird's new wax job appeared as liquid jewels dancing in the parking lot lights.

Tom dug deep into his right pocket and separated keys from pocket change as he shifted his load of cameras. He unlocked and opened the driver's door. Bending over, he extended himself into the car and placed his camera bags across onto the passenger's seat. He wondered all the while if it would have been smarter to load his bags through the passenger door.

When Tom attempted to move out of the car, his weight shifted, causing the car to move ever so slightly, disturbing the "liquid jewels" of water on top. Some of the beads ran together as they rushed toward the edge of the roof just above the driver's door, sloshed over the edge of the gutter and landed directly at the edge of his shirt collar. The cold water funneled down Tom's neck. He straightened up with a start. Since his head was barely inside the car, it didn't take long for a collision with the top to occur. Tom took several steps backward, put his hand on the back of his head, and muttered under his breath. Embarrassed, he looked sheepishly around to see if anyone was looking in his direction. Of course he realized at this time of night no one was. With a gentle toss, he sent his lightweight jacket into a pile on top of the camera bags in the passenger seat.

Tom maneuvered through the contortions necessary to get into his T-bird and closed the door.

"Sitting in a T-bird is a lot like just sitting down flat on the floor with your feet stretched in front of you, but once you're inside the fun begins," Tom reflected as he remembered thrilling times behind that steering wheel.

Tom switched on the ignition and flipped to start. The T-bird jumped to life with a mellow roar. The burned out glass packed mufflers and tuned stainless steel pipes enhanced the chugging sound created by the high-rise cam in the customized engine. But the car wasn't all sound. Very few '57 Thunderbirds could boast the power of this machine. From outside appearances, you would never know that this engine had been hopped up. The "sleeper" ran as good as it sounded. Tom seldom drove a car until the engine idled at least three minutes from the start to allow oil to coat the engine parts before putting the engine under a load. This gave him time to fasten his seat belt, turn on the lights and wipers, and tune the radio to the "oldies" station.

Tom flipped on the vintage radio and turned the dial...

> ..."T-bone steaks this week only...your cellular service meeting your needs...trade-in will never be worth more than it is today at...You people won't hear this anywhere but on this program, from this microphone. The mainstream media has gone brain dead."

As Tom heard the talk show host's fist pound the desk, he decided to listen for more. The host continued,

> ..." We at this program have received a copy of the Abrams Report, available to all the wire services and news networks in the country. I have it right here in my fingers. Nobody is saying anything about it but me."

The host intentionally rattled paper in the microphone.

...*"I'll tell you what the mainstream media won't. The Red Chinese army has built highways through the mountains of Burma and Tibet, highways capable of holding sustained loads of up to 150 tons. Why in the world would the Chinese communists go to such great expense to build a highway through those mountains? Well, I'll tell you why. A main battle tank and the truck that hauls it weigh 110 tons. The March II tactical missile and its launcher weigh 100 tons. The facts are, you people, the Chicoms have provided for themselves the means of moving an army to get at the riches of the world...fast. The Chicoms, for you people out there who are not savvy to political jargon, would be the Chinese Communists. The Abrams Report outlines a plan that would indicate a set up for an international incident in the Mideast. The plan is a conspiracy among North Korea, Iran, Syria, and China to generate an incident that would appear to be Israel's fault, thereby creating a spark which would ignite a Mideast war between Israel and the Arabs. With a billion people in their country, the Chicoms would have the ability to rush in and like heroes to stop the fighting. This would be their excuse to enter into Mideast oil fields with massive numbers of troops and capture the oil fields in all the Mideast, including Saudi Arabia. They'd hold the western world hostage, by withholding energy. The Chicoms need this energy to develop their country and bring it into the 21st century. They have already made progress in controlling worldwide shipping, such as controlling berthing rights on both sides of the Panama Canal and in other strategic locations around the world. The Abrams Report goes into a plethora of detail to explain the strategy of the Chinese plan. Your government and the mainstream news media are not telling you any of this. This is scary stuff, folks. You people better listen."*

"Wow, this is too heavy," thought Tom, turning the dial again.

"...Indianapolis Indians trounced the Omaha Royals 10 to 1 in nine innings of..."

"Ah, here we go," Tom said as he heard the last notes of one of his favorite oldies, then smiled as he heard the first notes of Sleepwalk. Tom hadn't heard "their" song in years. He thought it odd how a song can bring back so many memories.

As the music played, Tom's thoughts drifted back to a warm, spring evening and the Senior Prom. Many of the boys leaned against the wall on one side of the dance floor and some of the girls sat in chairs on the other side. "Wallflowers, they called us," Tom said aloud.

Tom remembered working up the courage to walk around the dance floor to the other side. The music was loud and the dancers were moving to a lively beat. As memories flooded back, he could almost feel the perspiration and the nervousness of anticipation as he made his way to the only empty chair at the wall, which just happened to be beside the most beautiful girl at the dance. The red ribbon flowing from her long, dark hair was a perfect match for her dress. The black velvet choker with the cameo in the center accentuated her radiant face and welcoming smile. Even now he could smell her sweet perfume. Tom felt his hands becoming clammy as he remembered asking her to dance. Tom took her hand and walked toward the bandstand to request a slow dance. The bandleader came over to take their request. The lead guitarist, the older and more mature of the group, stepped up to say he had the perfect tune in mind.

In a clear, deep voice, he announced to the other members of the band, "Sleepwalk...for Tom and Sharon!"

The guitarist's expertly trained fingers lovingly moved the slide along the neck of the guitar as he stroked the strings. The drummer created a soft background rhythm as Tom and Sharon stepped onto the dance floor. He took her in his arms as they danced to the slower music.

"How did he know our names?" Tom whispered.

Sharon offered no response. Their eyes locked together. It was mutual love at first sight! The melody played on. Soon the music faded away, then stopped completely. Tom and Sharon were the only ones who kept dancing…they were oblivious to their surroundings until giggles and chuckles startled them back into reality.

Sitting in the car listening to the music, Tom's face became flushed as it had been that night so many years ago in the high school gym when he and Sharon quickly got off the dance floor. Shaking the memories of the past, Tom said out loud. "After seventeen years of marriage, I love her even more!"

Tom backed out of his space and left the parking lot entering Capitol Avenue. The engine had warmed up and was really beginning to smooth out by the time he drove into the street. He drove south on Capitol and could see several traffic lights at the intersections ahead. The red, green, and yellow lights shimmered on the wet pavement. At this time of night, very few cars were moving down the street in that part of downtown Indianapolis.

The tires made a splashing sound as they ran through the water. The rain mist had stopped. That prompted Tom to roll down the driver's window to hear the sound of the engine echo off the steel and glass buildings all around him.

Tom thought, "Its times like these that make the car's rebuild expenses worth it!"

The car was over fifty years old and it cost Tom five times the original purchase price to overhaul and recondition it to showroom specs, plus a tweak here and there to hop it up a little.

Overcome by temptation, Tom succumbed to the desire to hear the engine roar one more time. While rolling at thirty miles per hour toward the red light, he slipped the gearshift into neutral and pressed down on the gas pedal. Instantly, the engine roared and the glass packs let out their beautiful highly tuned sound. The echo left chill bumps on Tom's arms.

"One more roar and then we quit," he said to himself.

And one more roar he got as he pressed down on the accelerator and then let up. He could imagine the glass panels in the buildings trembling from the sound. He touched the brake as the car rolled to a stop at the red light.

Tom dropped the gearshift into drive as the powerful engine

chugged to an idle. His childish grin showed that he was pleased with what he heard. Then he noticed another car pull into the intersection to his left and stop.

"Uh-oh," Tom said to himself, "the only other car I've seen since I left the office, and it has to be a police car."

In a second or two, Tom's light turned green. He hesitated, knowing that the police had to have heard the noise.

"Oh, man," he said as the smile left his face, "Am I going to get busted by the cops for loud mufflers?"

Tom pressed easily on the gas pedal and moved out slowly. Only a soft mellow tone could be heard. The two policemen had no reason to take special notice of a "cream puff" antique car. Little did they know it was a powerful "sleeper" with the rebuilt heart of a speed demon. They watched him pass through the intersection and stared in stone faced silence at the T-bird as it crept down the street like a scolded puppy with its tail tucked between its legs. Tom gave it a little more gas, sped up to thirty, and held it there.

Tom looked in his mirror and saw the police car make a left turn to follow him. "Left turn on red, huh? Guess cops can make illegal turns if they want to," Tom grumbled.

He continued toward the ramp up to I-70 West. As he drove onto the ramp, he noticed the police car make another left to go back into downtown.

"Whew," Tom said to himself as he breathed a sigh of relief. Instead of feeling like a responsible adult, he felt more like a teenager who had dodged a traffic ticket.

Tom pushed a little harder on the gas pedal. The T-bird quickly found sixty mph. Tom knew everybody added ten miles per hour to the speed limit. The highway at this point was only damp. With the tires singing on the pavement, pipes roaring, wind blowing in the open windows, oldies playing on the radio, the T-bird rolling west, and vacation coming up, Tom was loving life.

As Tom drove past the airport, he could still see storm clouds moving toward the northwest. Lightning continued to jump from cloud to cloud, nearly surpassing the brilliance of the downtown fireworks display on the Fourth of July. But the rapid frequency of intense electrical discharges within the clouds made the thunderhead seem ominous somehow, as if it were at war with itself. Concentrated bursts of lightning backlit one of the clouds revealing unusual shapes. A bright pinpoint of light, not unlike a distant fireball, propelled outwardly away from the thunderhead and into the night sky. Tom blinked, unsure of what he had just witnessed.

Off to the southwest, he could see the landing lights of a plane approaching the airport. "Aahhh, something I am sure of!"

Those landing lights reminded him of the times he and Sharon…oh, no Sharon. He had been in such a buzz talking to Sam at the office that he had forgotten to call Sharon to tell her he was on his way home. He usually did that when he was going to be late so she wouldn't be startled when he drove up to the house late at night. Tom could kick himself. He had left the cell phone in his truck. Nothing he could do about it now.

His thoughts moved back on track as he remembered the times he and Sharon drove with the top down while they watched for planes to land at the airport, then tried to adjust speed so that the car was directly under the plane as it passed over the highway. It was a lot of fun to be able to look straight up into the open wheel wells of the planes as they passed four hundred feet overhead. Just another game they played and another memory that he and Sharon had shared. The two of them had made many good memories.

Just past the airport, the speed limit changed to sixty-five. So Tom adjusted the speed to seventy-five. The isolated thunderstorms had left the pavement dry here. Traffic was unusually light. His car was the only one in sight going west. Tom could see the headlights of several cars going east. Those headlights were a great distance away, so he mashed harder on the gas pedal. The T-bird down-shifted and wasted no time getting to ninety, then ninety-five. Pushing a little harder, Tom raced the needle to one hundred five; with the highway still clear ahead, on to one hundred ten. Neither the engine nor the car strained at the speed. The oncoming head-lights went zipping by to his left. Now he saw no lights except for his own bouncing back from highway marker reflectors ahead.

Reluctantly, Tom let off the gas pedal to slow down to seventy-five. Listening to the pipes rumble as the engine slowed the car gave him a thrill. He waited for the needle to drop to seventy-five before he pushed the cruise control. Just another tweak Jim had added when he and Tom rebuilt the engine. Jim Newland was one of Tom's best friends since childhood. As his mechanic Jim was as proud of the car as Tom was.

The Plainfield exit sign flashed by. It wouldn't be long until the Highway 93 sign would announce that Tom was not far from home.

CHAPTER 2

Tom slowed the car to forty as he went down the ramp to Highway 93. A right turn at the end of the ramp sent him in a northerly direction toward the storm clouds. About a half -mile up the road the tires hit wet pavement again.

A respectable speed would be prudent now that the curvy and hilly road was rain slick, Tom concluded.

The radio had been crackling off and on as it picked up lightning bursts, which Tom knew was just the nature of AM frequency. Two miles from home, he noticed a strange buzzing sound in the radio. The static interference made it impossible to listen comfortably. He was compelled to turn it off.

Tom's concern for the radio was overridden by other unexpected events. The headlights were beginning to flicker as well as the dash lights. Several possibilities went through Tom's mind as he continued driving slowly. "There could be some malfunction in the electrical works. It couldn't be the ignition system, though. It's brand new. The battery's okay and all the clamps are tight, but that little high speed kick a few miles back on I-70… or high rpm in the street downtown… anything could have shaken something loose to cause a problem."

Tom made up his mind to take the car back to Jim's first thing in the morning, find the problem, and get it fixed before going on vacation. No sooner had these thoughts flitted through his mind, than the engine simply shut off.

"I could just kick myself," Tom muttered, "How could I have been so stupid? I'm not a teenager out hot-rodding a car! Now I've done it!"

Tom put the gearshift into neutral and coasted down the road. The headlights were dim, but he still had enough light to see the entrance to Arlin Brown's driveway. He pulled off the road onto the edge of the driveway, being careful not to block it. Tom got out of the car and just stood there, looking, trying to decide what to do first. He remembered that when he cleaned the car up he had taken everything out including a small flashlight and a tool kit. It didn't matter whether he found anything wrong or not; without tools and a light, he probably couldn't fix it.

Arlin Brown's two-story farmhouse stood atop a knoll that over-looked a meadow in the front which extended alongside the road several hundred yards. Behind the meadow and to the left of the house stood a small patch of woods. The house was dark.

"They must have gone to bed already. Matter of fact there are no lights at all up there. Don't they have a security light on a pole near the barn? Hmmm...must have been a power failure."

The house and barn were silhouetted against a background of stars. Since there was no moon, any kind of light was at a premium.

It suddenly occurred to Tom that the sky was clear above, but off to the northwest, he could still see lightning jumping in distant clouds.

"Well, what to do?"

Tom didn't want to awaken Arlin at that late hour, and since it was less than a mile from home he thought he might as well start walking.

"If I had the cell phone, I could call Sharon to come get me. She's probably asleep by now. Since today was her last day of school, she's probably exhausted. Teachers seem to need a lot of rest. That's one job I couldn't do. She puts up with more nonsense than I could stand. Sharon comes up with some real "war stories". Some of those kids would drive me crazy. But for some unknown reason, Sharon actually likes to teach. I'll just keep dealing with John Q. Public, if you don't mind. Everybody knows they're nuts."

Tom went around to the passenger's side of the car, unlocked and opened the door. He put on his jacket, gathered up his equipment, and locked the door. He walked around to the driver's side door and locked it. He looked at the car for a few seconds, being thankful that this trouble had happened only a mile from home and not in some unfamiliar place while they were on vacation.

As he started his walk home, he began to notice sounds of the night. Crickets chirped in the meadow to the right and leaves rustled on the trees in the woods to his left.

These mixed with the rattling sound of his equipment bags and his squeaking shoes on the damp pavement. Tom shuddered as an eerie feeling washed over him. The hair on the back of his neck stood up as he remembered the times when he and Jim as boys had dared each other to run through the graveyard late at night.

Tom, as a lone night traveler walked about a hundred yards to a gate leading into the meadow on the right. He looked over his right shoulder at the Brown's house, hoping to see some kind of light up there somewhere. He thought that if someone were awake and had a light on he would go back to ask for some help. But there was no light.

Tom was startled to the point of stumbling when he looked farther to his right. He noticed the parking lights of his car were on. The headlights were glowing dimly. "I thought I turned them off." Tom said aloud.

"Great! Now I've got to go all the way back to turn the lights off. If I don't the battery will be dead as a hammer in the morning." He muttered more under his breath about how stupid it was for him to walk off and leave the lights on. As if this chewing out he was giving himself would really help the situation. But it did take his mind off the night sounds.

As he approached the car, he noticed that the lights began to get a little dimmer, then brighter, then dimmer. "Oh, man! It's really messed up this time!"

By the time he got back to the car, Tom had already decided that two hundred yards of carrying equipment was enough. He went straight to the trunk, opened it deposited his gear and shut the trunk lid. He unlocked the driver's door, opened it and reached in to turn off the lights. To his surprise the light switch was pushed all the way in. It was already off!

"What made the lights come on then?" he wondered. "This is getting a little too creepy!" He walked all around the car and saw no lights on at all. He closed and locked the driver's door and headed off toward home once again, a little lighter and moving a little faster.

When Tom reached the gate again, he turned to look back toward his car to assure himself that things were as they should be. The car was still there with the lights off.

"How stupid of me to leave them on," he thought. "But wait… the switch was pushed into the off position. That still doesn't make sense. A BIG repair bill coming up," Tom grumbled in a low voice to himself.

Tom was walking sideways as he turned his attention from his car to the Brown's house on the hill a few yards from the car. The lights on the hill were still off. Tom thought the storm must have knocked out the power in the whole area. He zipped his jacket as he walked into the cool, damp night.

The noises in the woods to the left sounded like a popcorn popper as drops of water fell from the tops of trees to the bottom, bouncing the drops from leaf to leaf, as each drop splattered its way to the ground with a plop. Tom was startled by the sudden curious quiet in the meadow to his right.

A loud cracking sound split the relative silence.

"What was that? Where did that come from?" Tom asked himself out loud as he stopped in his tracks to listen for other sounds. Nothing…nothing. Not another sound. With his hands jammed into his jacket pockets, he walked briskly now, fully alert and poised to meet any threat, real or imagined.

"Funny how a sound in the dark can cause all kinds of things to go through your head," he thought as he dismissed the startling noise as a natural sound from the woods. "Woods are like that. They make noise for no apparent good reason."

He learned this a long time ago camping when he and Jim were Boy Scouts. However the urge to get on home seemed to be greater now. Forty years old or not, he really needed to be home. Crack! Craaackk!

Tom heard the sound again. This time it was much louder and

impossible to determine the source. Before he could actually look to his right, Tom saw a brilliant flash of light in the corner of his right eye. His hair stood on end once again, and the night lit up like day. Tom's first impulse was to dive headlong onto the ground. If this were a lightning strike, he didn't want to be one of the tallest things around.

Once face down on the damp pavement, Tom glanced to his right and discovered that it was no lightning strike. In the meadow, he saw an extremely bright rectangle as large as a movie theater screen. To Tom it appeared to be an enormous window of sorts. Through the window was projected an intensely bright beam over the meadow and across the road. It appeared to Tom as if it were an angry, giant florescent tube that had come to life.

The end of the beam struck the bank above the ditch at the edge of the woods on Tom's left. The light beam was making a sweeping move in his direction. It appeared to be about four inches above the pavement. As it moved, the fence posts at the edge of the meadow were severed in half. When the beam struck the bank, it ripped up dirt, rocks, sticks, roots, and grass, throwing debris in all directions. Its energy was like a localized miniature tornado. As heat hit moisture it made a sound like white hot metal being shoved into a bucket of ice water. It boiled, popped, screamed, and bubbled in a high-pitched crescendo of noise.

In that instant, Tom's main concern was for his own life. As low as the beam was to the pavement, he knew it would not pass over him if he stayed in the road. His only chance of escape was to roll over into the ditch to his left.

Tom tumbled into the ditch and met a bone-chilling splash. At least six inches of icy water had filled the shallow ditch.

While lying on his belly, with his head turned to the right, he held his breath. The whole fiery display above looked like a cutting torch had hit a piece of slag metal throwing sparks and balls of molten metal in many directions. The light display was not all that registered on his senses. A loud squealing like rusty nails being pulled from old dry hardwood, and the roar of rushing wind muffled the many other thumps and ground shaking thuds. He soon forgot about being cold and wet when he felt the heat from the beam as it passed directly overhead, within inches of his drenched body. The left side of his head and face were submerged in the ice-cold muddy water. For an instant he felt a searing pain on his right cheek causing him to take an involuntary breath. Tom coughed out a mouthful of water. Then he gagged, as he was suddenly overwhelmed by a horrible odor.

He held his breath again. Moments later the beam abruptly vanished.

For a few seconds longer, bits and pieces of rubble continued to plummet ending their violent flight. After that, the night seemed deathly quiet, punctuated only by the echoing sounds of dripping water in the woods nearby.

Tom could feel his pulse pounding throughout his body as his heart hammered in his chest. The cold from the water he lay in snapped him back into reality. With a gasp for air, he found himself repulsed once again by a putrid smell. Tom took only short shallow breaths to avoid the intense sulfuric, rotten egg odor. The air felt greasy from the lingering stench.

He could see an eerie glow on the trees to his left, reflecting a lower intensity light source coming from his right. He stayed still in the water for what seemed like an eternity. It was actually no more than a few seconds. Slowly and cautiously, Tom raised his head. Looking to his right he could see more of the light source as he raised himself higher in the ditch to look out over the road surface. He did a slow push up in the ditch, extending his arms beneath him into the frigid mud and leaves. He stretched up his neck like a turtle to see all he could without rising too far from the relative safety of the ditch.

Tom could see a very strange sight in the blue-white glow in the meadow. His first impression of the bright rectangle appearing as a movie screen was confirmed. It looked exactly like a movie screen but was suspended in mid air. For an instant it appeared as if he were watching a movie... but this movie was real! It had depth...real depth! Tom could see shapes moving about inside the screen. As he watched, a shadowy figure emerged from the darkness, and then ran into the screen the way someone would go through an opened door. Immediately upon its entering, the whole bizarre scene vanished.

As Tom's eyes became accustomed to the darkness again, he could faintly see glowing embers from the burning twigs lying all around. The smell of scorched wood now intermingled into the heavy odor laden air.

Tom inched his way onto the roadway. Lying face down on the pavement, he looked around, in bewilderment, assessing his situation. For about a minute he listened and looked, wondering if it were safe to try to get up. Hearing or seeing nothing else to alarm him, Tom cautiously rose to his feet.

He noticed that the storm clouds had moved even farther away. He could still see an occasional flash of lightning in the ever more distant clouds. Looking straight above he could see bright stars in the sky. Tom knew for certain what he had experienced the last few minutes was no lightning strike. His mind felt traumatized as he tried to assemble the bits of information.

"Couldn't be lightning, not from a clear sky! But what was it? And what was that screen?"

Shivering, he took his first steps toward home. Except for the crunch of the rubble in the road as he walked and the squish from the water in his shoes, it sounded as if the night was back to normal. But the nasty odor reminded him that it wasn't normal. Tom replayed the whole scene in his mind. His thoughts ran in many directions, like a handful of BBs rolling in a metal trashcan. Nothing made sense. He suddenly felt a real sense of urgency to get home.

It was hard for Tom to tell if his shaking came from cold shivers or from being nearly scared to death. Socks and shoes soaked with muddy water didn't add anything to his comfort level. On he sloshed, looking this way and that wondering what might spring at him next.

Tom walked, then jogged, then ran as his sense of urgency to leave the area increased. Fresh air again filled his lungs. He passed the woods, then the open fields on both sides of the road. With only a quarter of a mile to go, Tom slowed to a walk. Things were beginning to look normal. Even the bugs were singing their usual nighttime chorus. A gentle breeze stirred the air around him. He shivered again.

Tom wondered if the surreal scene he had just left could have been a hallucination. His cold, wet clothes reminded him that it was not.

A sense of relief swept over Tom when he saw the entrance to his driveway. Remembering he didn't have the garage door opener with him, he squished his way to the back of the house. The security light sprang to life as he rounded the corner. He stopped at the back door of his garage. He entered a code into the alarm keypad and opened the door. Once his shoes were removed, he reset the alarm and listened for the musical note that announced the alarm was armed. He walked through the laundry room and stepped into the hall. Tom was suddenly reminded how cold he was. His body continued to shiver and his teeth clattered so much he could scarcely call out Sharon's name. On his way to the bedroom, Tom glanced into the den to see the clocks in the VCR and stereo both flashing 12:00.

"Sh Sh Sha...ron!" he called out....

"What?" came a sleepy reply.

"Sharon, I was scared out of my wits tonight!" Tom said as he passed through the dark bedroom and made his way to the bathroom.

Sharon was more awake now. It wasn't Tom's routine to come into the house late at night making so much noise. Tom didn't usually come in this late at all.

"Did you get caught in one of those storms that passed through?" Sharon asked sleepily as Tom fumbled for the bathroom light switch.

"Wait till I get out of these wet clothes," he said as he started taking off his pants.

Tom flicked the light switch while looking in Sharon's direction. As he moved into the now lit bathroom a startling sight appeared in the mirror above the sink.

The sight unnerved him. He jumped back, lost his footing, and found himself lying askew on the bathroom floor, still unsure of what he had seen in the mirror.

The commotion in the bathroom completely awakened Sharon. She sat up in bed with a start. She called out for Tom as she rushed toward the bathroom to see what had happened.

Sharon helped Tom get to his feet. Her mouth fell open in disbelief as Tom leaned toward the mirror for a better look. They both got a close look at his face.

Sharon shouted in a panicked voice. "What has happened to you? What's that smell?"

"I don't know..." was Tom's almost whispered reply.

His face looked normal on the left side but appeared to have a serious sunburn on the right. A line ran from the base of his throat, dividing his chin, lips and nose. It continued across his forehead separating normal color skin on his left from the bright red on his right. Most startling, the line continued into his hair, separating normal from strange. It was as if the pigment had been vacuumed out of his hair on the right.

Tom and Sharon stared at the image in the mirror before them.

"Tom, what happened?" Sharon cried, her voice trembling from fear.

"I don't know. It was something like lightning, but it wasn't lightning. I don't know what it was. It was bizarre and it was close."

"Tell me, tell me, tell me!" Sharon pleaded.

"I'm all right." Tom reassured her as he shivered while changing from the cold, wet clothes.

Tom was convincing, and, as Sharon's fear began to subside, she asked, "Are you hurt? Do you think you need to see a doctor?"

He touched his face with his fingers. He felt no pain...not even a slight tingle. Except for the discoloration, there was no sign of injury. "I don't think so. It looks like a burn, but it doesn't feel like one. I don't know what it is."

"Looks like a bad sunburn to me. Tom, tell me what happened!"

Tom wasn't sure what had happened so he stalled her with, "Honey, let me get out of these wet clothes and into a hot shower, then I'll tell you the whole story."

On the walk home, Tom had considered the possibility that the strange encounter at the meadow was some kind of nightmarish dream, or that whatever caused him to dive into the water filled ditch was just a hallucination. The changed appearance of his face in the mirror convinced him. Something real had happened. He didn't know what...he needed time to think.

Tom removed the rest of his wet and muddy clothes then tossed them into the hamper. He climbed into the steaming, hot shower. He relished the idea of standing under the soothing water as it warmed his chilled body.

"Tom, did you wreck the car?"

For the first time since this ordeal began, Tom felt amused. "No," he laughed, answering over the noise of the shower, "but it broke down in front of Arlin's place. I walked home from there. I'll tell you all about it when I get out of the shower."

A few warm minutes later Tom turned the water off and opened the shower door. Sharon had placed his robe, pajamas, and towel on the chair. Tom picked up the towel, dried off and dressed. As he combed his towel- dried hair, he examined his scalp in the mirror. No scalp burn. He could hear Sharon making rattling noises in the kitchen.

Two steaming mugs of hot chocolate were waiting on the kitchen table. Tom savored the idea of warming his insides as he remarked to Sharon that he felt a lot better.

Without commenting on that statement Sharon said, "I've waited long enough. Now tell me the story."

Tom replayed the story starting from the time he left the interstate until he got home. Sharon was as bewildered and alarmed as Tom was. When he finished they both sat in shocked silence for a long time contemplating.

Sharon broke the silence with, "Tom, you must tell someone about this. I don't know who, but someone. What happened to you isn't normal. It's unnatural, unreal."

Tom replied with: "And have them send the guys with a straight jacket to take me off to a rubber room somewhere? No thanks!"

Sharon looked at the clock on the kitchen wall. It was 1:25 A.M. The adrenaline burst they both had experienced was gone now. Tired and sleepy feelings were creeping in. They thought of bed. After all they had both been up since 5 A.M. It had been a long day.

Tom and Sharon made their way to the bedroom. They hung their robes on the bedposts and climbed into bed, snuggling together under the sheets.

In a few minutes, Tom said in a sleepy voice, "I did something else earlier tonight."

"What was that?"

"I listened to Sleepwalk on the radio."

Simply the mention of the song spirited Sharon back to the night they fell in love. She saw the transformed gym, the bandstand, the red and gold streamers hung from the rafters. She relived the moment she saw Tom as he hesitantly walked around the dance floor. She watched the guitar player as he announced the slow dance just for them.

"You listened to Sleepwalk without me being there?"

"No, you were there all right." Tom answered as they snuggled closer together.

CHAPTER 3

R ING-G-G-G.
The shrill sound jarred him from a deep sleep. Not fully awake, Tom threw his hands up in front of his face to protect himself from the beam.

RING-G-G-G.

Tom turned quickly to defend himself from the sound that came from his right. Awakening he realized he was not under attack, as Sharon reached across him to answer the telephone. Knowing that it was only a phone did nothing to slow his racing heart.

"Hello," Sharon said, sleepily, as she pulled the phone across Tom's chest to her side of the bed. From the sluggish sound of her voice, it was obvious to the caller she had been awakened.

"Mrs. Alexander?" he asked.

"Yes."

"This is Sheriff Carter. I'm sorry to wake you up, but I need some information."

"OK. What information?"

"Do you own a red '57 Thunderbird?"

"Yes we do, but my husband had mechanical problems with it last night. I'll let you talk to him"

"Tom, it's the sheriff," Sharon said as she handed the phone to Tom.

"The who???"

Tom had recovered from his initial adrenaline rush. He was

somewhat calmer now, but his heart was still pounding as it had the night before.

"Come on, honey, take the phone."

"Hello," Tom said, trying to make his shaky voice sound calmer.

"This is Sheriff Carter. I'm sorry to wake you. Can you tell me why your car is sitting on the side of the road less than a mile from your house?"

"Yeah, it quit running on me. I got it out of the road as far I could. Why do you ask? Is there something illegal about where I left it?"

"No, it's not that," replied the sheriff. "Your neighbor Arlin Brown reported some odd occurrences near his house and your car is part of them."

"Odd occurrences? Let me tell you about odd occurrences!"

"You can do that?"

"Well, I...."

"Can you come back to your car now and shed some light on this situation?"

"Funny you should mention light."

"What?"

"Never mind, I'll tell you when I get there. Just give me a few minutes."

"I'll be here," said the sheriff.

Before Tom even had the phone back on the table, Sharon was tossing clothes in his direction. Neither of them were very concerned about what they were wearing. Sweats would work. They dressed and headed toward the garage.

"Wait a minute," Sharon called to Tom. "You can't go looking like that!"

"Looking like what?"

"Your face...your hair!"

"What's wrong with my fa...Oh!...yeah."

"People will wonder what happened to you!"

Tom grabbed a baseball cap. "Come on, let's go!"

Sharon climbed into the passenger side of the Ford Explorer, and pushed the button to raise the garage door as Tom slid under the steering wheel. While Tom backed out, Sharon pushed the button to lower the door, scarcely noticing the musical note that sounded as the door shut.

The drive to the T-bird didn't take very long. It was still dark at 3:05 in the morning with no hint of daylight. In the dark, details of Tom's experience from the night before were not visible to the eye. However the red and blue strobe lights on two police cars pierced the darkness. One police car was parked at the entrance into the meadow. The gate was standing open. About two hundred feet from the road near the center of the meadow, three men with bright flashlights were intently studying something.

As Tom sped past the gate, the tires crunched debris on the road. He hastily pointed out to Sharon where he had rolled into the ditch the night before. Tom swerved into Arlin's driveway and parked behind the police car. He and Sharon quickly walked toward the people gathered a few feet away. The red and blue strobe lights flashed on Tom's face.

"What happened to you?" Arlin asked in amazement. In the flashing lights it was evident that Tom's appearance was not quite right.

"See, I told you people would wonder!" Sharon reminded Tom.

The sheriff did a double take and blinked when he saw Tom's face.

"It's a long story, but basically, I almost got struck by lightning or something."

"I've never seen lightning do THAT to anybody!" the sheriff said. "You must have really been close."

"I was," Tom answered. "But I'm not sure it was lightning."

"I hate that I had to ask you to come back over here this early in the morning, Mr. Alexander," said Sheriff Carter, "But after what Arlin reported to us, we seem to have a lot of questions and no answers. Did you say that you had car trouble and your engine wouldn't run?"

"Yes."

"Then why is your engine running now?"

"What?" asked Tom, with a quick look in the T-bird's direction.

Tom hadn't paid any attention to the engine noise he heard. He assumed it had come from the police car. All four people walked over to the T-bird. He could hear the powerful chug. The engine was running. Tom reached down to open the door. It was locked. He asked the sheriff to check the passenger's door. It too was locked. Tom retrieved the keys from the ignition in the Explorer.

"I don't understand this. The engine was not running when I left the car here." Tom went on to tell the sheriff about the trouble with the light switch, that the switch was off and yet the lights were on. The sheriff had another piece in a strange puzzle.

Tom unlocked the driver's door and eased in under the steering wheel. He reached over to unlock the passenger's door. Sharon was kneeling on the ground beside Tom in the open driver's door. Arlin and Sheriff Carter bent over at the passenger door to look into the car. The sheriff aimed his flashlight into the car. The beam illuminated the ignition switch. It was in the off position. Yet the engine was still running. Tom had the keys in his hand.

"What's going on here?" Tom asked perplexed.

He put the key into the ignition switch and turned it to the on position, then back to the off position. The engine quit running.

They all looked at one another without saying anything. Tom turned the key to the start position. The car started right up as if nothing had ever happened. He switched the key back to off. The engine quit. This was repeated three times. The results were the same.

Tom checked the lights and radio. Everything worked as it was supposed to.

"I don't get it," Tom said, after climbing out of the car.

"I don't either," the other two men related at the same time.

"It seems we have ourselves a mystery here," the sheriff said. "Some time after Arlin's power went off; he got up to get a drink of water. When he looked out the window above his sink, he saw a brilliant flash of light in the meadow over there. When his eyes got used to the dark again, he saw two figures running toward the far side of the meadow in the direction of the woods. He also saw someone a few minutes later moving down the road toward your place."

"When I got closer to the window I had a better angle of view and I could see the end of my driveway," Arlin added to what the sheriff had said. "That's when I saw your car, Tom. Something didn't add up, so I called the sheriff. I didn't want to call your house and scare Sharon without knowing what was going on."

"I really appreciate that," Sharon acknowledged.

"That someone on the road was probably me," Tom said. "But I didn't see anything or anybody running toward the woods. I did see something running into a brightly lit area in the middle of the meadow."

Tom was interrupted when one of the deputies shouted from the meadow. "Hey sheriff, you better come over here."

All four left the cars and headed toward the three flashlight beams that were now fixed upon one spot in the meadow.

"What do you make of this?" one deputy said as they got closer.

"What is it?" Sharon exclaimed.

One of the deputies said, "It's definitely not human, but it doesn't look like any kind of animal I've ever seen!"

They all speculated on what the creature might be. Everyone had an opinion, but no one knew with certainty.

Tom noted aloud that he had never seen anything like it before. Everyone agreed.

"Maybe if the body weren't cut and burned so badly, we could tell more about it," Arlin commented.

"We need to get pictures of this!" Sheriff Carter announced.

Tom said, "Wait a minute and I'll get a camera." He headed off to get his cameras out of the trunk. He found them just as he left them. After selecting two cameras, he shut the trunk and returned. He handed the 35mm camera to Sharon. The other was the digital camera he used for newspaper projects. They each took several pictures.

"Hey, look at this," the sheriff shouted, as he bent near the ground. "It has what looks like a chain around its neck. Take some pictures of it!" Sheriff Carter had moved the creature's head with a stick to expose a chain.

After a closer look, Tom could see that in fact it was a shiny chain. To Tom it appeared to be made of gold. One link was spread open as if something had been removed. Tom took several close-up pictures with the digital camera.

One of the deputies speculated that it looked like an ID tag had been pulled from the chain. Another deputy noted that most ID tags he knew of weren't placed on a gold chain.

The sheriff instructed one of the deputies to call for the coroner to bring his equipment and pick up the creature. "We'll take it to his lab for examination. Maybe he can tell us what it is."

Tom looked at his watch and said to Arlin, "I've got 35 minutes to meet a deadline with these pictures. Do you mind if I use your computer to transmit these digitals and a story?"

"No problem. I'll go up with you."

Like many mid-western farmers, Arlin used advanced technology to manage his 1,000 acre farm. Instant information access as well as satellite imagery was available at his fingertips.

Tom and Sharon went to the cars. Sharon drove the Explorer with Arlin in the passenger's seat and Tom followed in the T-bird. They drove into the grass and around the police car, which was parked in the driveway. The grass beside the driveway was neatly mowed. Tom's T-bird with its low clearance had no problem navigating the short turf.

They drove on up the hill near the house and parked their cars. As they neared the house, they were met with the smells of fresh brewing coffee and frying bacon.

Tom took his equipment straight to Arlin's computer room and tossed his cap on the desk. He removed the wires from his camera bag and connected the camera to the computer. He transmitted the digital pictures along with a brief summary of some of his activities of the night before, drawing no conclusions and promising updates and an exhaustive investigative report for later publication. With the touch of a key, his report was transmitted via the Internet to his editor's office at the Hoosier Tribune.

Tom was totally unaware that powerful surveillance computers had locked on to one word of his message, triggering an avalanche of events. Little did Tom know this transmission would change their lives dramatically.

"How many police cars are down there, Arlin?" called a woman's voice from inside the kitchen. "I need to know how many eggs to cook."

"Two cars, four guys, honey," was Arlin's reply. "I'll go tell them to come on up here." As Arlin went back outside, he noticed that it was nearly daybreak. They would be able to get a good look at things soon.

The deputies had gathered at the sheriff's car by the time Arlin walked down to the foot of the hill. He was met with grins all around when he extended a breakfast invitation to the men. The sheriff posted one deputy to stand guard over the creature while all the others followed Arlin to breakfast.

Maggie Brown had hardly looked up from her cooking when Sharon came into the kitchen. She was busy trying to manage three skillets of bacon, sausage, and eggs. Sharon helped by taking over the bacon skillet. For a few minutes the two women engaged in cooking talk.

Maggie turned to look in Tom's direction, when he entered the room, gave a startled gasp, then asked, "What on earth has happened to you, Tom?"

Not knowing how to describe the previous night's events, Tom replied, "I don't know! It could be a near miss from a lightning strike. I just don't know," Tom replied.

"What else could it be, Sharon?"

"We just don't know, but he doesn't seem to be hurt. He just looks dreadful."

Arlin, the sheriff, and his men had washed up and drifted into the dining room where they heard Tom and Maggie's exchange. The deputies hadn't paid much attention to Tom's appearance out in the dark. Their attention was drawn to the creature they had found. Only now did they observe how strange Tom looked.

Tom could feel their stares and turned to announce to everyone, "I'll tell the whole story at breakfast. Oh, by the way, Arlin, thanks for the use of your computer. I made the deadline."

"Any time, Tom."

When breakfast was ready, they all sat around the dining room table to eat. Conversation around the table centered on the many happenings of the night before. Most of the banter was speculative; each person offered a bit of opinion on what had taken place.

They finished their meal. Everyone bragged on the breakfast as Maggie poured more coffee. They relaxed back into their chairs as Sharon and Maggie cleared the table.

"OK, Tom, let's hear your story. I need to make a report," said Sheriff Carter.

Arlin, with Tom's permission, had placed a tape recorder on the table. Tom was glad he did. He thought he might want to hear his own story replayed sometime.

Tom told the same story he had told Sharon the night before. All the others listened without saying a word. Sharon watched Tom's audience intently, reading their facial expressions. After the questions were asked and Tom's "I don't knows" were said, the men decided to go check the scene since it had become daylight. The view from the top of the hill gave them a better perspective of the scene below.

"Hey! Look at this!" Tom exclaimed. "You can't see all this stuff from down there!"

"Man, what a mess!"

"Wow!"

"What on earth did this?"

The blackened and wilted grass made it evident that heat had caused the damage. They observed that a single pivot point from the middle of the meadow had formed a strange pattern.

"Looks like the work of a giant windshield wiper."

A groove was cut in the bank above the ditch at the outer edge of the pattern on the other side of the road. To the observers it appeared to be about six inches wide and 90 feet long. Grass was scorched in the meadow. Everything taller than one foot, including fence posts, was mowed down. Dirt and debris were strewn about. All this destruction was consistent with the sweeping action of the light beam that Tom described earlier.

After a thoughtful pause, Arlin asked Tom, "What did we see here?"

"I don't know, but I'm taking pictures."

Tom took all his cameras out of the trunk of the T-bird and handed them to the deputies. He went back into the house and retrieved his digital camera, then joined the others at the foot of the hill. Tom walked to the entrance of the meadow just as the coroner's van pulled up. The old coroner was in the business of seeing odd things, so he wasn't much impressed with Tom's appearance. To him Tom was just another weirdo in the crowd.

Sheriff Carter joined the coroner after he parked his van along the side of the road near the meadow. They walked together to the body of the strange creature. The coroner preformed the first real examination there in the meadow, giving no explanations and having no answers.

For the next hour detailed reports were written and more than a hundred pictures were taken. This information would be the focus of many a round table discussion.

The sheriff and his deputies wrapped up the initial investigation and drove back into town.

Sharon had called from Maggie's kitchen to schedule a 9:30 appointment with Dr. Randall for Tom. Since it was nearly 8:45, Sharon urged Tom to hurry.

After cameras were secured in the Explorer, Sharon started off toward Jim Newland's garage. Tom followed in the T-bird. He expected the car to quit running at any time, but it didn't. The little car ran as well as ever.

Jim's garage was just a short distance on the other side of I-70. They took the first road to the right past the interstate and drove a fourth of a mile to Jim's place on the left.

Jim Newland was one of the best mechanics in the state of Indiana. He commented about the burn on Tom's face. Tom told highlights of the bizarre tale again. Jim listened with interest at every word. He asked several questions for which Tom once again had no answers.

Jim's appointment schedule was tight but he promised to take Tom's car right away. He told them that if he found anything wrong, he would fix it as soon as possible. They climbed into the Explorer and left, heading east on I-70 to the doctor's office.

Dr. Randall was ready for them and promptly at 9:30, he called them into his office. "Goodness!" the doctor remarked. "What have you been into?"

"It's a long story, doc, but I think it could be a flash burn from lightning." Tom used the lightning story to avoid a detailed explanation. He could only guess what it really was that had caused his burn. The expression on Sharon's face as Tom spoke confirmed that she too doubted the lightning story.

"Well," Dr. Randall said. "It does appear that the redness is caused from a pigment change, but there is no evidence of a burn and no damage from a burn. I don't understand that, nor do I understand the loss of hair color. If you look closely, you can see that the hair has lost color only on the outside area of the hair mass." He used a tongue depressor and lifted the white hair to expose darker hair underneath. "There seems to be no burn on the scalp either. I think that a fairly close haircut will take care of the difference in hair color. You may want to try some of Sharon's make-up on your face. If you have any other problems with this, don't hesitate to call me."

Tom and Sharon finished their business with the doctor, stopped at the pharmacy to purchase make-up for Tom, and then went to the barbershop. Everywhere they went Tom was asked about his appearance. Tom was uncomfortable with all the unwanted attention. He would be glad to get rid of the conversation piece. The barber got almost all the white hair cut out. The little that remained was hardly noticeable. Sharon assured him that the make-up would fix the redness problem on his face.

Tom gave her a quizzical look but he understood that he would have to wear make-up for a while if he wanted to stop the strange looks he was getting.

It was almost noon. The tired couple set out for home. The day's vacation plans would have to be on hold for a while.

As they passed by Arlin Brown's house, all seemed normal, except the debris in the roadway and the cut-off fence posts. The police cars were gone. No one could have guessed the excitement of the last twelve hours.

Tom glanced to his right to look over at the meadow as they passed. He suddenly slammed on the brakes and came to a stop. "Look at this!" he said to Sharon as he put the Explorer in reverse. Tom backed up twenty feet or so quickly, and then slowed to a crawl, still backing up and looking at the meadow.

"What did you see?" Sharon wanted to know.

"There!" Tom said as he hit the brake again.

"There what?" Sharon asked while looking at the meadow.

"See the grass mashed down?"

"Not really," Sharon replied.

Tom pulled the Explorer as far to the right of the road as he could, turned on the flashers, got out and walked to the fence. Sharon followed him.

"Look at the grass, honey," Tom said. "Notice the difference in the way the sunlight hits the blades and they reflect the glare. The grass with glare is undisturbed... the dark spots are footprints where the grass has been mashed down."

With that explanation, Sharon could see what appeared to be two sets of footprints leading to the edge of the woods behind the meadow.

The footprints in the grass were boldly evident to the two of them. They realized all this wasn't born from the power of suggestion.

Tom got out one of his cameras and finished the roll photographing the footprints. During the end of the fifteen minutes they were at the side of the road, Sharon and Tom watched the footprints disappear. The angle of the sun had changed and the glare was no longer visible.

"Wow!" Sharon exclaimed, "Was that pure chance or what? If we had been fifteen minutes earlier or later, we would not have seen those prints. Where did you learn to look for stuff like that, anyway?"

"Uncle Sam's army," Tom replied. "Did I ever tell you about digging spider holes?"

"No, but I'm sure you're going to."

"A spider hole is a small fox hole with a lid. When you carry the dirt away to hide it you have to be careful not to walk on grass or you'll bend it over. And you never walk in the same place twice. You can draw a map to your hiding place if you don't watch where you step."

"Gee, that does make sense," Sharon thought. She wondered how many other things the 82nd Airborne had stuck into her husband's head. "So Arlin really did see two figures running toward the woods last night."

"Looks like it," Tom murmured as he concentrated his stare into the woods. He saw nothing unusual. "Come on, let's go home."

"I'm ready," Sharon replied wearily as they climbed into the

Explorer and drove away.

Once inside the garage, the musical note sounded letting them know that the door was down and again they were secure.

Shortly after 1:00 P.M., they dropped into bed for a nap. Sleep came easily to the exhausted couple; despite the uneasiness they felt from the mystery beginning to surround them.

CHAPTER 4

A fter a short nap, Tom stretched and yawned on his way to the kitchen, where Sharon had set out coffee and sandwiches.

As they finished up their last few sips of coffee, Sharon found herself wondering where their vacation trip might take them this time. Just for the sake of adventure, Tom and Sharon had a tradition: they flipped coins to determine the roads to be traveled for short trips. No advance plans could be made and they really didn't know where they were going. The coin tosses that determined which direction to go could be exciting or disastrous, often exciting, she thought as she remembered past trips.

As if he could read her thoughts, Tom wisecracked, "I hope our coin flip takes us somewhere away from the crowd so I don't have to keep explaining my face. Explaining redness is one thing, but explaining make-up is something else again."

"I've been thinking," Sharon said. "Why don't we go straight to Mom and Dad's cabin this trip? It's nice and quiet, not crowded with people, and you wouldn't have to explain your face burn. And, anyway, wouldn't a fish fry be fun?"

"Hmmm, fish fry! I can smell it now. Sounds like a winner. Call your Mom and Dad while I take care of the kitchen. We can check on the T-bird on our way."

Tom was finishing in the kitchen when Sharon came to tell him that everything was set to go to her parents' place. The cabin in the hills between Dayton and Cincinnati had water, electricity, air conditioning, telephone, television, and other amenities. It could be as primitive as a sleeping bag beside a campfire at the edge of the lake or it could have all the comforts of home all at the flick of a switch. The cabin rested at the edge of a patch of woods alongside a man-made lake fed by a cold freshwater stream. The lake was stocked with blue gill and large mouth bass with a few catfish thrown in for good measure. The stream that fed the lake was known to have some pretty big rainbow trout. It was decided. This would be a good trip.

They left in Tom's pick-up to make the quick trip to Jim's garage. As they drove past the meadow, they met an oncoming black Mercedes idling along slowly at about the spot where Tom rolled into the watery ditch. The Mercedes' windows were heavily tinted, but through the opened driver's window they could see that the occupant was talking on a cell phone as he looked over the meadow area.

"Oh, well," Tom thought as he and Sharon passed. "It's a free country. People can look if they want to. It does seem odd, though!"

Tom pulled into Jim's driveway. The T-bird was rolling out just as they drove up.

"Hi, Tom," Jim said. "You got here just in time to pick this baby up."

"Did you find out what was wrong?"

"What I found out was that there was nothing to find. This is the best-tuned car I've seen in quite a while. The electrical system, gas lines, battery, everything checked out perfectly. Don't want to sell it do you?" Jim added.

"No way," Tom replied. "I do need to give it a bath though. That's the only thing wrong with it. A little rain sure can make a mess, can't it?"

Tom got into the T-bird and started down the country road. Sharon followed in the truck. It appeared to Tom that Jim was right. The car purred like a kitten. Tom was glad to be back on the road again and anxious to get everything in order for their trip to the cabin the following day.

The next morning, feeling refreshed from a full night's sleep, Tom once again did his customary immaculate clean up ritual on the T-bird. Covered with highway rain spray and dirt when he started, it sparkled like new money when he finished and drove it into the garage. With the help of the ceiling mounted winch, a grunt, and a tug, Tom removed the hardtop from the car and placed it in its storage rack in the garage. He pulled the vinyl top from the boot behind the seats and checked to be sure it was clean and working properly. They planned to drive with the top down but had to be prepared for sudden rain. Tom remembered all too well the time the vinyl top wouldn't come out of the boot and they both got soaked.

As Sharon watched his endeavors through the kitchen window, she knew the car was running a close second to her. "My maintenance requires a bit more than the car's," She thought. Sharon's upkeep was not nearly as extensive as most women's. Her beauty was natural, needing little attention. She had kept herself fit and trim, maintaining the same figure she had when Tom fell in love with her. Exercise and eating healthfully were part of her daily routine. With her clear, creamy complexion and smooth skin, she used little make-up. Her dark hair required nothing artificial to keep it that way. Sharon was the kind of person equally at home teaching a classroom full of English majors, working in the garden or attending a symphony. She could hold her own in debates with colleagues as well.

Sharon was nearly living her dream life except that in her dream she would be watching their child helping Tom clean and polish the T-bird. Tears came to Sharon's eyes as she imagined what might have been, but the doctor said was not to be. She had resolved that their lives would be full without children, but in moments like these she couldn't help feeling empty.

Shaking off those feelings, Sharon finished in the kitchen, then hauled the suitcases out of the attic and began packing. Choosing what to take was a bit of an art when traveling in the small sports car. The suitcases had to be big enough to hold the things they needed but small enough to fit in the T-bird's trunk.

Tom loaded the luggage into the car. He showered and dressed, then made one lap around the house, going through a mental check list to make sure the stove was turned off, doors were locked tight, windows were shut and locked, light timers were set. He patted himself on the back for remembering the cell phone from Sharon's car. He didn't want to be caught without it again. As they climbed into the T-bird, Tom's last mental note was to see that the Explorer and the Ranger were in the garage; the garage door was down and locked and the alarm was set. Then they were off!

The first order of business was to stop at Steve Nicholson's house across the road. Steve and Linda, along with their son Andy, had agreed to look after Tom and Sharon's place while they were gone including collecting the mail. Tom and Sharon had done the same thing for the Nicholsons when they were vacationing. They had peace of mind knowing that the place was taken care of and that the house looked lived in.

Tom and Steve had known each other for several years. They had served in the 82nd Airborne together. Tom's last job in the army was as a 1st Lieutenant, acting Company Commander, a captain's job. Steve was one of his platoon sergeants. Steve was a "lifer", a 20-year man. Tom, on the other hand, stayed only four years after graduating from college and ROTC. He had made good use of those few years, however, excelling in carrying out his responsibilities. Tom preferred the simple life he had now over the high stress job of military excellence.

The two men served together in the Second Gulf War, and there forged a special bond between them. Tom and Steve were among the first to be put at risk. The 82nd and the 101st Airborne Divisions were the first American units sent to face Saddam Hussein. It was a token line of defense at first, two battalions from each American division against Saddam Hussein's five divisions of Republican Guard, reinforced with infantry. The American "pucker factor" was way up until reinforcements arrived. If the Iraqis had made a sudden move to attack, they would have rolled over the Americans as if they weren't even there. The reputations of the 82nd and 101st airborne divisions caused Saddam to hesitate. By the time he realized his mistake, it was too late. The Americans arrived with enough military might to hurt him badly.

Tom reminisced. Operation Iraqi Freedom is history but the bond of friendship created between him and Steve during those times of life and death was a solid bond, firmly cemented by one specific incident.

First Lieutenant Thomas Alexander and Master Sergeant Steven Nicholson, by rights, should be dead. As military objectives of Operation Iraqi Freedom were accomplished elements of the 82nd Airborne Division maneuvered into advance positions. The war seemed to be over. Tom's unit dug in and quickly established a security perimeter at its furthest point of advance. Company commanders were ordered to report to their battalion command posts for a briefing. Tom requested Steve to accompany him. They hitched a ride on a Humvee loaded with a much needed supply of fresh water. Traveling across desert wasteland, Steve and Tom held on firmly as the driver dodged rocks, holes and gullies. At one point Tom suddenly ordered the driver to stop so he could inspect the third platoon's defensive position. He and Steve stepped out of the Humvee. Tom directed the driver to continue and told him they would hitch another ride later. About 50 yards down the road the Humvee detonated a hidden Iraqi anti-tank mine. The trooper driving died instantly. Tom and Steve were spared. Steve felt he owed his life to Tom's spontaneous decision. Normally Tom would not have made that stop. His orders were to report to Battalion CP ASAP. For some reason, Tom felt compelled to make that particular stop at that particular time.

Most people experiencing near death situations together go their separate ways, but not Tom and Steve. They stayed in touch. When Steve was nearing retirement at the end of his 20-year enlistment, Tom learned the small farm across the road from his house was going to be offered for sale. He knew it was meant for Steve.

It was winter when the Nicholsons moved into the sizable old-fashioned farmhouse. Tom spent many hours that first winter helping Steve tune his ham radio equipment. At first the off frequency radio transmissions interfered with the neighbors' TV reception. They spent several winter nights eliminating the problem. Later the only evidence of a radio transmitter would be the 75-foot antenna tower in Steve's backyard.

The native North Carolina family did well adjusting to Indiana farm life. Steve's retirement income from the army was more than sufficient to support his family. Profits from the farm were used to purchase expensive survivalist equipment.

Of all his survivalist procurements Steve was most pleased with the twin cylinder diesel generator, which sat in an innocent looking storage building a few feet from his back porch. In the loft above the generator sat a thousand gallon fuel tank. That much fuel would allow the generator to run for a very long time supplying electricity to the house. The "icing on the cake" for the generator was the remote starter that Steve had bought from a junk car dealer. At the touch of a button he could start and stop the diesel engine from inside the house, eliminating the need to go out into a cold Indiana winter night to provide emergency electricity.

The generator powered everything in Steve's house including the deep well pumps that supplied water for general use and for the reverse osmosis water filters. Fiberglass storage tanks in the basement contained several hundred gallons of the purest, cleanest water around. Basement shelves stored canned and dried food as well as medical supplies. To the casual observer the Nicholson's basement looked like a military surplus store.

Steve had his boundaries though; the armed camp stayed in the basement. Linda was adamant. She would not allow the upstairs to be anything but a home for her family. There were no guns on display and no military supplies. Antique furniture, throw pillows and doilies were the order of the day for the living area. Even though Linda insisted on having a sanctuary from all the survivalist equipment, she believed in her husband's desire to be prepared for anything.

Their son Andy had expressed an interest in the army and Steve wanted to teach him all he knew. So they made up games of defense and played them around the farm. Some of these games Steve had learned in the army and some he created. From time to time the neighbors could hear gunfire coming from the ravine at the rear of the Nicholson's farm. They knew that Steve and Andy were conducting target practice. Steve was aware that any piece of equipment they owned would work during a true emergency because it had worked dependably during the games they played regularly.

They worked hard and played equally hard. They wouldn't

know until later that one of their games would play a significant role in their future.

Most of the neighbors considered Steve to be a survivalist nut; however, they rested easier knowing there was a man like Steve around. They knew that Steve's only concern was for the safety and well being of his family.

Tom stopped the T-bird on the shoulder of the road at the edge of the Nicholsons' manicured yard. Steve and Linda had been in Michigan at a band competition with Andy for a couple of days and were playing catch up with yard work. All three stopped what they were doing to talk with Tom and Sharon. Sharon handed Linda their mail that she had collected while they were away from home. Once again, Tom saw questioning expressions as the three studied his discolored face. Before he could begin his explanations, their attention was turned in the direction of the road.

Arlin Brown's car was speeding toward them. He slowed to an abrupt stop behind the T-bird.

As she and Arlin jumped out of the car Maggie shouted, "Look at this!" She waved a newspaper in the air. "Tom's story and pictures made the front page."

"You know, Tom," Arlin commented, "I've heard your story first hand, but it seems to pack more punch when you read about it on the front page of the paper."

"What's going on?" Steve asked.

The Nicholsons hadn't heard anything about Tom's story and were completely uninformed about the unusual incidents that had taken place. Tom wished he had the tape recording he made at Arlin's house so he wouldn't have to repeat the story. But since he didn't have it he related the strange tale one more time for his friends. The Nicholsons reacted with the expected amazement.

After Tom's retelling everyone's curiosity was heightened and they gathered around the hood of Arlin's car while Maggie spread the paper out. There on the front page below the fold was an unedited version of Tom's article and two pictures of the creature that he had sent to the paper the day before.

"Those guys in the news room got right on this story," bragged Tom.

As each person read the article, the Browns and Alexanders filled in the gaps with the Nicholsons on what happened two nights before.

"Strange stuff, huh?" Arlin said to Steve.

"I'll say it is!"

It was Andy who noticed the National Press headline and article in the paper above the fold. "Dad," Andy said, "does this mean that you and Tom will have to go back to the army?

"Let me see that!" Steve said.

He and Tom read the article together. "Iranian, and other Muslim fundamentalists, threaten to annihilate Israel if certain Jewish practices at the Wailing Wall do not stop." It was apparent from reading the article that the murderous Islamic suicide bombers and Israel's retaliation against them were secondary in the hearts and minds of the Arabs when it came to religious considerations. The article went on to say that if Israel did not stop provocative actions concerning the Dome of the Rock Mosque in Jerusalem, Iran and other Islamic nations would unite and take military action to stop threatening gestures being made toward Islam. The article continued to say that Iran was not an Arabic state, but the Iranians were presently the most militant nation in the Mideast. The report added that Iran's Muslim ties with nations such as Iran and Syria could be used to whip them into a bloody fervor against Israel. The article did not specify the details regarding what had ignited the Iranian and Palestinian anger, stating only that the Jewish practices at the Wailing Wall and the recently discovered plans for the rebuilding of the Temple at Temple Mount were the source of dispute. The Muslims consider Temple Mount their third most holy place. To the Jews, Temple Mount is the most holy place on earth. The two religions are adamantly opposed to each other. The article concluded by explaining that the United States had a military agreement to defend Israel in the event of attack.

"Well, son, I certainly don't want to go back to the sand oven; do you Tom?"

Tom answered, "No way do I want to do that again!"

"I'll second that," Sharon chimed in.

For the next few minutes the topic of conversation was the

unusual front page of the Hoosier Tribune.

"Wonder what's going on?" Tom asked aloud as he chased memories of desert heat and wartime stress through his head. "You know, before the beginnings of the First and Second Gulf Wars, there were similar rumblings in the Mideast, then a month later we were at war. We can read about it today and be shooting at each other tomorrow...or maybe we're already shooting at each other and the general public doesn't even know about it. But then who knows?"

"Why would a weekly newspaper be printing this kind of stuff, anyway? None of the other newspapers are reporting stories like this one. In fact the only other place I've heard anything like this is from a radio talk show host," said Arlin.

Linda asked, "Is the Hoosier Tribune trying to get out of the weekly and back into the daily real news business?"

"I just write the articles and take the pictures," Tom answered. "I don't have a clue to what management is doing. Anyway, gang, vacation's waiting, we've got nearly 200 miles to drive and we're burning daylight!"

Sharon smiled at Tom's remark. She knew Tom stole this "burning daylight" statement from one his favorite John Wayne movies.

"Here, have this newspaper for light reading," Arlin said as he tossed the paper into the T-bird.

"Take care of things while we're gone," Tom shouted as the engine fired up. They waved good-bye from the open convertible as they sped down the road on their way toward I-70 east.

"Do we take I-74 to Cincinnati or go to Dayton on I-70?" Tom asked Sharon.

"I'll flip our quarter to see." Sharon reached into the ashtray and pulled out the vacation coin. "I-70 it is." Sharon announced after flipping the quarter.

"Either highway between here and the cabin is a bummer, anyway," Tom complained. "It's been in a constant state of repair and reconstruction for at least six years. It seems that some construction company and the state have turned the project into a career opportunity. They maintain a constant construction project. They've already spent enough time and money to build the highway from scratch."

Sharon jokingly reminded Tom that he had already spent his allotted "gripe time" for the day.

Tom chuckled, "You're right."

They traveled the concrete ribbon of highway through downtown Indianapolis, mingling with heavy traffic as they caught waves from other classic car buffs. Swirling puffs of wind ruffled their hair and lightly massaged their faces.

Like kids with a shiny, new toy, Tom and Sharon treasured the time they spent traveling in their T-bird, especially with the top down. Even with a clear view of the sky above, they were unaware of three helicopters flying directly overhead, at a high altitude and traveling in a westerly direction. They were most certainly unaware that Tom was the reason the helicopters were there.

The Alexanders didn't notice the helicopters, but the Browns and Nicholsons did. They were still talking at the side of the road when from out of nowhere, shattering the peace and quiet, roared three U.S. Army Apache helicopters flying at tree top level. Their sudden arrival and loud noise was both startling and unsettling. To the unsuspecting spectators on the ground, these Apaches were loud, fast, and frightening. The roar diminished as the helicopters moved farther away.

Steve had seen them in action before in wartime situations. "Those choppers are Apache Longbows. That's a model OH 58 D. I worked with those in the army. See that ball above the rotor?" Steve pointed out that each helicopter had a large basketball shaped unit mounted above the main rotor. He continued by telling Arlin that the units contained highly sophisticated electronics used to find and scan targets.

"I'd know a Longbow anywhere. You wouldn't believe what they can see with those things! Those machines could hover behind a tree line with the ball barely above the trees and the chopper crew could see for miles. They can't be seen because the trees hide the body of the chopper," Steve explained.

Steve continued to extol the virtues of the Apache Longbow. The meadow and the woods between the Alexanders and the Browns appeared to be their target area. Steve recognized the criss-cross search pattern they were flying. He could tell from seeing the missiles mounted on the helicopters that they were loaded for bear. Somehow he felt this was no game.

"It's too dangerous for them to be flying around heavily populated areas in choppers with that much firepower aboard," Steve told the others. "Something isn't quite right here."

Andy brought out a pair of binoculars. They all spent the next twenty minutes watching the helicopters travel back and forth, gradually working a little farther away with each pass. Steve speculated that the reason for so many helicopters was that each machine had a different set of scanning devices and all were covering the same ground. Steve explained to them that infrared and ultraviolet capabilities, night vision and classified technologies were at the crew's disposal.

"Those things can pick up a heat source like a human body hidden inside a house and display an image of that body on a TV screen in the chopper," announced Steve.

The helicopters worked farther and farther away and finally disappeared from sight. Arlin and Maggie said their good-byes to the Nicholsons and left. They drove past the Alexanders, and then as they approached the meadow near their house, they noticed a black Mercedes parked at the gate into the meadow. Since the windows were so darkly tinted, it was difficult to see if there was a person in the car.

But there was a person in the car...a very determined person...a person whose mission was initiated by a strange sequence of events.

Without his knowing, Tom's article and digital picture transmission via Internet to his office downtown had triggered Project Deep Blue into action. At Project Deep Blue, located at Ft. Meade, Maryland, there were 125 super computers linked together to scan the World Wide Web for key words in Internet transmissions. Words such as bomb, assassinate, plot, alien, UFO, etc. were words that activated Deep Blue. When Tom described the beam of light as an "ion beam" in his article, the computers locked on. This trigger phrase caused Deep Blue to retrieve the whole transmission. It was scrutinized by project managers who would determine its worth for investigation. The man at the meadow in the black Mercedes had found it worthy.

By the time Arlin drove his car up the hill to their house, got out, and looked back down, the Mercedes was gone. It apparently wasted no time getting out of sight.

Farther down the road, however, the Nicholsons had walked back up to their porch. They hadn't gone into the house when all three noticed the black car pull slowly into the Alexanders' driveway and up to the house. A tall, slender man with dark hair and a dark suit got out and made his way to the front door. He rang the doorbell and stood there as if waiting for someone to answer, but all the while he was observing as much as he could through the window. Steve watched as the man attempted to force the door open. When that didn't work, he closely examined the window. He then discovered the security system and stopped his entry attempt.

The Nicholsons observed the stranger as he walked toward his car, then suddenly turned to go to the back of the house. At this point they lost sight of the man.

"I don't like the looks of this," said Steve. "That man is trying to break in. Get the laser rifle, Andy. We'll execute Delta 3. Remember to be careful. Do it the way we practiced. Don't let him see you!"

Andy understood immediately. Delta 3 was a war game they had practiced often.

Steve went ahead of Andy as they crossed the road directly in front of their house. The two disappeared behind a fencerow that bordered the Alexanders' property. They were able to get across the fencerow behind the vegetable garden. Andy took up a position against a potato hill just behind two rows of corn which were about two feet tall. All he needed was an opening through the plants to see. He was not visible from the Alexanders' house as he lay on the ground with the rifle pointed at the dark suited man now standing at the back door. Andy was apprehensive because he was having trouble seeing the laser dot on the man's dark jacket.

Steve walked quietly through the grass between the garden and the house. He was watching the man feverishly try to subvert the alarm system by inserting random codes into the keypad. Steve stood still about thirty feet from the man's back, watching him. Steve had been careful in approaching the house so that his reflection did not appear in the door glass, giving his position away.

After watching the man for a few seconds, Steve said in a loud, but distinctly Southern voice, "Hey! What do you think you're doin', mister?"

The man at the door was startled and spun around suddenly. His suit jacket came open to expose the harness to a shoulder holster under his left armpit. Andy could clearly see the laser dot on the now exposed white shirt. The man's right hand moved in an upward motion.

Again using a loud voice, Steve said, "You're a dead man if you touch that gun!"

The man's hand stopped reaching for the pistol as he noticed the red dot on his shirt. He slowly let his right hand come back to his side. He wondered why this "hick" was talking so big since he had no weapon. The red dot indicated that the "hick" had a partner. The partner had a weapon but was nowhere in sight. The trespasser's steely eyes shifted from place to place frantically trying to locate the weapon.

"Don't move even a little bit till I tell you to! You'll kindly take notice of that red dot on your shirt."

The man looked down at his shirt. He already knew what the red dot was. Steve told him anyway.

"That's a laser gun sight, my man. The red dot is where the hole will be made when the thirty caliber hollow point goes in and then your back opens up like an exploding watermelon. Be real calm right now because my partner has a nervous trigger finger."

The man nodded his head in acknowledgment.

Steve said in a deliberate tone, "Now real slow, take the gun out of the holster and put it on the concrete right at your feet."

The man did as he was told.

"Now back away real slow till I say stop."

Without taking a step, the man said, "I'm just going to pull out my ID card."

"You do what I tell you to! Now!"

The man complied.

When the man had taken ten steps, Steve told him to stop. Steve picked up the pistol and allowed him to reach for his ID. The man reached into his jacket pocket and brought out a leather case that apparently held an ID card.

"Put the ID down on the concrete and kick it over to me."

The man again complied.

Steve and the man just stood looking at each other for a few seconds, each one sizing up the other. The dark suited man kept trying to locate the gun that was trained on him. He couldn't find the gun's hiding place. He was afraid to take his eyes off Steve, and more especially his own .45 pistol Steve was holding.

The man considered his situation. A stranger had captured his weapon. A laser sight from an unknown location had marked him as a target. He decided it was time to be meek mouthed.

"I'm a federal agent."

"I don't care if you're the Pope! If you're trying to break into someone's house around here and you don't have a search warrant, you're in trouble! Now you just stand there! Don't move and keep your yap shut, you hear?"

Again the man nodded. Steve read the card inside the leather case. "J.T. Williamson, agent United States of America, Central Intelligence Agency. Well I'll be dipped! A CIA man operating within the boundary of the United States. Well, J.T. or whatever your name is, do you think the people in the state of Indiana are stupid? Or that we don't know what the Constitution says? Do you think we believe that the CIA is allowed to have operatives within this country…and where do you get off trying to break into this house? Did you ever hear of the 4th Amendment?"

"Look, mister," J.T. said. "This is a matter of national emergency."

"Yeah, that's what they say when the feds get caught breaking the law…you got anything to do with the choppers that went over scaring the daylights out of everybody?"

"Yes, as a matter of fact, I do have something to do with it. We're using the Apaches to try to apprehend a couple of desperate fugitives. They were sighted in this area. The reason I was trying to open the door was to see if they were hiding in the house."

"Oh, yeah! Now that's a believable story!"

J.T. was obviously agitated. Steve didn't know if this story was the truth or not. He took the card out of the case and put it into his shirt pocket.

Steve told J.T. to stay put while he unloaded the pistol. Steve took the magazine out of the handle and checked to see if there was a round in the chamber. There wasn't. At least this dummy had enough sense not to chamber a round in an automatic pistol and carry it around that way.

Steve put the magazine in his pants pocket and said sarcastically, "The government's got plenty of .45 magazines and I need another one so I'll keep this one if you don't mind."

Steve told Andy to stand up and come over to him. Andy did as his dad instructed. J.T. was shocked to learn that a mere child had held him at bay. Andy kept the rifle trained on J.T.

"Move on out to your car now," Steve said.

They all walked to the car, Steve watching the red dot and Andy at a respectable distance with his finger poised at the trigger. Steve ordered J.T. to open the trunk. When the lid was up, Steve tossed the empty pistol in the trunk and shut the lid. J.T. got into the Mercedes. Steve ordered him to put all the tinted windows down so he could see into the car.

"You know I really should have you arrested right now for that stunt you tried to pull. Next time you come snoopin' around, bring a search warrant and the sheriff."

J.T. backed his car into the road and headed toward I-70, relieved that he wasn't on his way to jail. Andy and Steve watched the Mercedes disappear out of sight.

Linda was a nervous wreck. She had been watching Andy through the binoculars while he was in the garden. She could just barely make out the top of his head as he kept the gun sight on J.T. She couldn't see Steve from her viewpoint, but she could plainly see what went on in the front yard as J.T. left. Even though Linda was a bit apprehensive for her son, she was confident that her husband could take care of himself. After living with an infantry paratrooper for 20 years, she had peace of mind. Steve had stared death in the face before and was trained to react to it. When Andy and Steve got home, she met them with a barrage of questions. Many of her questions had no explanations.

While relating the incident to Linda, it occurred to Steve that if the government sent men with millions of dollars worth of hardware to hunt for two desperate guys, they must really be desperate. Something just didn't stack up. Steve mentally kicked himself for not holding the man called J.T. until the sheriff could check him out for the attempted break in.

"There really might be something to his connection with the choppers." Steve thought.

Steve called Arlin and consulted with him about the afternoon's tension-filled events. After listening intently to what Steve had to say, Arlin agreed that an opportunity was lost in not holding J.T. The men concluded they should assume that there were dangerous fugitives in the area and to take appropriate precautions. Steve and Arlin agreed that the situation was serious but would downplay it somewhat to calm their families. They made arrangements to be watchful and keep each other informed of any other unusual events.

Meanwhile, many miles to the east at the I-75 intersection with I-70, Tom turned south. After driving at a leisurely pace and making several stops along the way, they found the exit that would take them to their vacation spot. Soon they saw the familiar sign at Toby's Market. They stopped for supplies, and then hurried on toward the cabin before it got too dark. As they got closer to the cabin, the landmarks seemed more familiar. It had been almost five years since they had been there. Not all that much had changed. They drove down the winding country road. At the end there was an almost unnoticeable but very neat gravel driveway that led to a patch of woods. After driving a short distance through the woods, the cabin appeared in a clearing just ahead of them, perched above the bank leading down to the edge of the lake.

A cool breeze blew through the woods and across the lake. Woodsy smells met them as Tom parked the car near the front door. Sharon found the key in its hiding place, opened the door onto the screened porch, and went into the cabin.

Tom located the hammock and strung it between two trees as Sharon made a light supper. When the meal was finished, Tom lit a camping lantern and put it on its hook at the edge of the porch. A light wind felt refreshing as it carried in unfamiliar smells. They climbed into the hammock and shared together how peaceful it was there around the cabin and the lake and how much they needed this rest. Before they knew it they had drifted off to sleep. After a couple of hours sleeping in the hammock, a chill awoke the two and they retreated to the warmth of the cabin.

The quiet, calm atmosphere that met the couple that night would soon be shattered. Unknown to them, very soon their lives would take a drastic turn.

CHAPTER 5

It was late in the day and after business hours. All the employees at the Hoosier Tribune had gone home for the day, except for Sam. He was doing his usual fastidious job as night custodian. While he worked he listened to the radio that could be heard all over the office. Sam enjoyed listening to Dixieland jazz. It seemed to make time pass more quickly. After a couple of hours of work, he decided to take a breather. He poured a steaming cup of coffee from his thermos, and then settled in at Tom's desk to take it easy. He leaned back in the chair, put his feet on the desk and gave his full attention to the music.

There was a disadvantage to playing the music, however. It covered up the sound of the front door locks being picked. It covered up the sounds of the squeaky hinge. It covered up the sound of footsteps in the lobby. Sam was unaware that anyone was around until he heard a loud voice say, "Get up Alexander!"

With a start, Sam swiveled around in the chair. He didn't even notice the hot coffee that spilled down his shirt as he dropped the cup. He looked into the face of the man known to others as J.T.

Sam's eyes dropped to the hand that held a .45 caliber automatic pistol. Sam knew to check to see if the hammer was pulled back. It was. If a round was chambered, and the trigger was pulled, the gun would fire. That settled any notions Sam may have had about being heroic.

"I said, stand up Alexander!"

Sam got to his feet, raising his arms up at the elbow with palms open to indicate that he had nothing in his hands. "I'm not Alexander," he said nervously.

"Don't give me that!" J.T. snapped. "Who do you think is stupid here? The name on your desk and the name on your parking space are telling me that your name is Tom Alexander, and you're the man I'm looking for."

Sam suddenly regretted having taken Tom up on his offer to use his desk and parking space.

"I want the medallion!"

"I don't know what you're talking about, mister," Sam pleaded. "I'm not Tom Alexander. He's on vacation!"

"Just shut up and give me the control medallion now! And turn off that stupid music!"

"What medallion? Mister, I don't know what you're talking about." Sam replied his hands shaking as he turned off the radio.

"You know what medallion; the one you pulled off the gold chain that's in your pictures."

"I don't have pictures! I don't have a medallion! I don't know what you're talking about! I'm not Tom Alexander! I told you! He's on vacation!"

"You're lying, Alexander!"

J.T.'s anger was becoming more visible as he made a swinging gesture with his pistol. A strange expression came over Sam's face as he thought he was going to be shot.

Sam grabbed his chest in pain and dropped to his knees. Puzzled, J.T. watched as Sam crumpled face down onto the floor.

"Heart attack. Great. This guy dies on me and I'll never get the medallion!"

He felt for a pulse and found none. Sam was clammy and lay very still.

"This is not my day," thought J.T. as he reached in Sam's hip pocket for his wallet to check his identity. As he read the driver's license, he muttered to himself, "How about that? He's really not Alexander!"

J.T. pulled the drawers out of Tom's desk and dumped the contents on the floor. Tossing the drawers aside, he rummaged through the piles, searching…searching… searching….nothing.

J.T. decided he had pressed his luck far enough. As he left the building and walked toward the Mercedes, he looked around to see if there was anyone who could identify him. He saw no one. He drove slowly out of the parking lot and into the street so as not to draw attention to himself.

"Where could that medallion be? Could this guy Alexander have taken it with him on vacation? Surely not. It must be at his house."

J.T. blended into the rest of the southbound Capitol Avenue traffic and faded into the night that covered the city.

Sam stirred a little. He had pain in his left arm and chest. Ever so slowly, he managed to get to the edge of Tom's desk. He pulled on the telephone cord and the phone fell to the floor with a clatter. He managed to punch the 911 buttons but could not speak into the phone. The effort of the last few minutes was too much. He faded into unconsciousness.

"Hello…hello…hello…" the operator kept repeating but got no response. The 911 call triggered an automatic caller ID, which informed the operator of the source of the call. In a matter of minutes, a police car was at the front door. After a careful entry through the unlocked door, the policeman slowly made his way into the lobby, then into the office area. He observed empty desk drawers on the floor tossed in among piles of dumped contents. He saw Sam's feet from around the edge of the desk. Not knowing what to expect, he ducked back into the lobby area and pulled out his pistol. He used his radio to call for backup, while looking over the office area to see if anyone else was there. Seeing no one, he lay down on the floor to see under the desks and again saw no one.

With the pistol still in his hand, he crawled to Sam's side. By the time he checked Sam's pulse, more police and an ambulance had arrived. The paramedic noted that Sam now had a pulse, but it was weak. It would be a short run to the hospital but they had to hurry. A few minutes later hospital attendants met the ambulance at the emergency room doors. The ER doctor was called and a good cardiac specialist soon saw Sam. The faithful custodian would have the best of care.

The police called the newspaper's managers back to the office to help with the investigation. It was obvious that Tom Alexander's desk wasn't torn apart by accident. They concluded it was not a normal robbery attempt. Sam's wallet was still on the floor with money inside. Other valuables in clear view were left undisturbed. The police investigators were puzzled as to the purpose of the break in. If not for money and valuables, then for what? They hoped that Sam would shed some light on the situation later when he was able to talk.

After leaving the Hoosier Tribune office building, J.T. drove directly to the coroner's office. Deep Blue had discovered in Tom Alexander's intercepted computer message to his newspaper that the unidentified body found in the meadow had been taken to the coroner's office. The locks were easy to pick. The contents of the heavy black plastic bag that he had stowed in the trunk of his car would tell no tales. J.T. thought to himself, "At least that part of the assignment went right. After all who would want to break into the coroner's office, much less steal something out of a cooler?"

J.T. glanced at his watch. 8:32. He was an hour ahead of schedule in meeting his boss at the airport. His mission at the coroner's office had gone quickly. However, he was troubled that the black Mercedes might be becoming connected with his growing list of crimes. He felt the need to hide the car. He didn't want to kill time just driving around. J.T. entered a crowded parking lot at a shopping mall on the south side of town.

While sitting in the car J.T. studied the shoppers going about their business. Families were shopping for summer items: bags of charcoal, lawn chairs, pool supplies. Sometimes J.T. longed for the life he never knew. He tilted his seat back to a relaxing position and turned on the radio.

> ... *"the alphabet soup news networks won't tell you this stuff, the only place you'll hear the truth is through the Abrams Report, right here on this program. The Abrams Report's accuracy rate is phenomenal. I'm telling you now; you'd better pay attention! They're exposing some serious stuff. The Red Chinese Army has amassed troops along its*

Eastern China coast. That much everybody knows. The reason for this amassing of troops has been unclear. But at noon today, the Abrams Report divulged intercepted Red Chinese Army intelligence. These intelligence documents disclose a multi-faceted plan. One phase is to create a diversionary military move in the Mideast. The second phase is to suddenly involve Taiwan and North Korea. These documents also insinuate that there is a third phase, which could be an invasion of Japan. The objective of the third phase is unknown at this time. The Abrams Report concludes that these Chinese plans may be only the tip of the iceberg pertaining to Red Chinese Army ambitions. You people had better listen up out there! The Abrams Report is strongly suggesting all out war! If only half the stuff they're telling is true, we're in big trouble!"

J.T. had heard enough. "That guy always rants about something!"

The radio was distracting him. J.T. turned it off. He had problems close at hand to worry about. He didn't have time to ponder what the Chinese were doing.

J.T. began to analyze the day's events. When he picked up his boss at the airport in two hours, he knew that he would be held accountable for his successes and failures. Successes would be expected and be met with no comment, but he knew he would get ripped for his failures. He had failed in his attempt to locate the gold control medallion.

"Alexander knows where that medallion is. I wonder if he knows the significance. I bet he has it in his house. It sure wasn't at his office."

J.T. wondered about the old man that he had mistaken for Tom at the office. He hadn't intended to kill him. "Dead men give no information. Why did the old man have to have a bad ticker anyway?"

J.T.'s mind wandered. Suddenly, he had a brainstorm. "Why didn't I think of this before?" he muttered to himself as he locked the car and went into the mall just like any other shopper. In a few minutes he returned with a large package and placed it in the back seat. He looked at his watch. It was time to move again. He slowly drove out of the mall parking lot, into the street, and proceeded toward the airport. At the airport he found his boss waiting in the passenger pick up area. Instead of a suitcase, J.T.'s boss held only a briefcase. The man got into the car with J.T.

"Hello, George," J.T. said.

"Hello, nothing," George replied. "This is the worst run assignment you have ever done. You and the Apache team both struck out! You didn't get the medallion and the coroner's office has the sample, thanks to a nosey sheriff who shouldn't even have been on the scene. You should have been there sooner."

As they pulled away from the curb, J.T. ground his teeth and thought, "I was right. George didn't waste a second before he got to my chewing out. He's an ill-tempered nut. He needs to get a real life." J.T. knew George always breathed fire down subordinates' necks when he perceived anything short of a perfect mission. This time George was not one hundred percent correct in his assessment of the situation.

"Just wait a minute George," J.T. said. "In the first place I got there as soon as I could. I can't help it if a neighbor called the sheriff. And in the second place, the sample is in the trunk. So, the entire mission wasn't a flop."

"You got the sample?" George quizzed. "How did you get it?"

"I simply picked the lock on the coroner's office after they had all left for the day, went in and opened one cooler after another until I found it."

"You're getting good at this breaking and entering stuff, aren't you?"

"Do I detect a compliment?" J.T. thought. "Naaah, no way, not from this guy."

"Well, maybe there is hope," said George as he glanced over his shoulder observing the large box in the back seat. "What's the chain saw for?"

"I have a plan," J.T. said. "I'll need your help."

As the Mercedes blended with other traffic in the crowded area around the airport, J.T. discussed his plan with George.

"I can't get my hands on the medallion this Alexander guy took. The old man at his office claimed he's on vacation and who knows where. That house of his has the security of Fort Knox, except for one small place. It's my job to find other peoples' weakness, and I found his. This is where I need you and the chain saw."

J.T. laid out the details. George liked the plan. They checked the time. It was little more than five hours until J.T. had to get George to the rendezvous point. They had time for the plan to work. George was on a mission for his boss too. That mission was to gather all the things that J.T. collected, and then deliver those items at a prearranged pick up point at 4:30 A.M. But the problem was J.T. hadn't collected all the items. He needed the gold medallion.

They drove to a remote gas station. J.T. opened the trunk to get a box out. His nostrils flared and he grimaced at the stench beginning to accumulate in the trunk. The odor from the unrefrigerated sample was beginning to leak through the plastic bag. J.T. fished out a pair of dark brown coveralls and gave them to George.

"Go to the restroom and put these on." J.T. told George. "I'll make do with this dark sweatshirt."

When George returned from the restroom, he and J.T. quickly assembled the chain saw. They bought gas and oil and poured the mixture into the tank, sloshing a bit on George as they went. After three pulls on the rope, the saw rattled to life as it belched a cloud of white smoke. The two men grinned at each other. They knew that the job was going to be easy.

The station attendant began turning out lights and closing up as they left. After a short drive, they found the entrance ramp to I-70 west. They noted the time as they drove. It was 1:30 am. Three hours should be plenty of time to get the job done and go to the rendezvous point.

* * * * * * * * * *

Steve Nicholson was a creature of habit. Some of the habits he learned in the army would never be broken. One of those habits was to observe his surroundings before he went to sleep. Every night he would walk outside to look into the night and just listen, checking for anything unusual. From the front porch, he took particular notice of Tom and Sharon's house. Since no one was home it was his duty to take care of his friends' property. Noting nothing unusual, Steve stepped back inside his house, locking the door and turning out the lights as he went. Because of the possibility of two fugitives in the area, Steve was restless and was making his nightly rounds a second time that night.

Steve walked to the back of the house and onto the back porch. He looked and listened again for anything unusual, taking special notice of the fields around the back of the house. He neither heard nor saw anything out of the ordinary at this time of night. This was Steve's ritual. It was such a part of him that he was hardly aware of doing it. Whether it was the muggy heat of summer or the bitter cold of Indiana winters, the ritual was the same.

He shut and locked the back door without knowing how close he had come to making a major discovery. If only he had made his rounds in reverse order, he would have been on the front porch in time to see the black car with its headlights turned off as it crawled up the narrow gravel road that led past the Alexanders' property. He certainly would have heard the tires softly crunching gravel as the car made its way ever so slowly through the darkness. But Steve was at the back of his house, not the front.

As the car crept to a stop the two government agents rehearsed the plan. While still sitting in the car, both men put on dark gloves and ski masks, not so much to hide their identity, but for camouflage. Immediately upon opening the door the two men realized they had made a huge mistake. They had forgotten to tape down the door light switches. The interior lights in the car would show up like a lighthouse beacon in the black of night. They had to act quickly, but quietly. They grabbed the equipment box and chain saw from the back seat and got the doors closed quickly. Once outside, J.T. reached into the box and retrieved two sets of starlight goggles, which would enable them to see in the dark.

J.T. led the way through the knee-deep grass near the edge of the field. George followed with the chain saw. Both men bent at the waist and stayed as low as possible, moving quickly toward the garden near the rear of the house. J.T. had already told George about the trouble he had faced in that backyard from an overzealous military nut. They didn't want a repeat episode. The security light in the side yard was the biggest problem. During his earlier visit J.T. had determined that an approach from the east end of the house would avoid the scrutiny of the motion detector that triggered the security light. With that in mind, the two men dashed across the open yard to the back wall of the house.

J.T. also learned earlier that Tom's security system was a good one with a complicated code for the keypad. However, even the best security system couldn't protect completely if the installers didn't identify all the points of entry. J.T. had found the Achilles heel. The crawl space door was unguarded.

J.T. smugly congratulated himself for his discovery. He was well experienced in finding loopholes in other peoples' plans. He knew an average run of the mill burglar would not even have looked for a crawl space opening. J.T. was not an average run of the mill guy. He was the type who would stop at nothing to accomplish his task. He would even walk away and leave an innocent man at the point of death and not bother to make a simple phone call for help.

George, on the other hand, didn't like to dirty himself with the details of normal operations, but he was first to take the credit for any of their successes. He enjoyed his position of trying to manage employees such as J.T., whom he considered to be among the "get down and get dirty" kind of people. He was well trained in the art of subversion, and used people like J.T. as tools of the trade. He would be pleased to take credit for finding the gold medallion in this house after J.T. finished his chain saw work.

These were the kinds of people that Steve looked for every night in his vigilance to protect home and family. That night, years of dutiful observation almost paid off.

Carefully J.T. moved the cover off the crawl space entrance and lowered himself into the opening. He removed his goggles and ski mask, laid them aside, and took the chain saw from George. On hands and knees he moved through the crawl space until he reached the area he estimated to be under the center of the living room. He used his small penlight to double check the controls on the saw, then inserted earplugs and waited for George to give the go ahead.

George still smelled of gas fumes from the clumsy spill earlier that night. As he began his descent into the crawl space, he mentally noted that he was glad odor detectors were not part of home security systems. On his knees, with his head and shoulders up out of the hole, he surveyed his domain like a desert prairie dog. He watched carefully and listened intently for several seconds. Observing no threats, George closed the crawl space door. He removed his goggles and ski mask and put in his earplugs. He then signaled with his penlight to start the saw.

With one pull on the rope, the engine fired up with a deafening noise. The confined area of the crawl space compacted the noise and the smoke. The job had to be done quickly.

George thought how ridiculous this situation would seem to an OSHA inspector: "Two government employees working on the job in a dark confined space using dangerous equipment that made a lot of noise, spewed smoke like a steam engine and could cut a man in half in a flash...OSHA would have a fit. But then those guys don't mess with the CIA much anyway," George concluded.

J.T. pulled the throttle wide open and jammed the chain bar into the plywood floor above. The saw kicked as the teeth grabbed wood. He held on tight. A hard shove sent the saw through the floor, showering the living room with wood chips and carpet pieces. Like using a hot knife in butter, he quickly sawed through the dry plywood and 2x12 pine joists. Sparks flew in the darkness as the chain teeth hit nails. In just a few short strokes, a four-foot square hole appeared in the living room floor as panel along with carpet came crashing into the crawl space.

J.T immediately shut off the saw. Even though he used earplugs, his ears were still ringing. Both men were coughing after inhaling the heavy concentration of smoke. The entire cutting process took an amazingly short amount of time, less than 90 seconds.

George opened the lid to the crawl space just enough to get his head through to the outside. He didn't want any smoke to get out and give them away, but he had to check to see if everything was ok outside. He had taken his earplugs out and put the goggles back on.

He looked around for about a minute, saw nothing and ducked back into the hole, closing the door as he went. He made his way to the hole in the living room floor.

Smoke preceded the two men as they climbed out of the hole and into the living room. The smoke from the chain saw exhaust set off the smoke detector in the hall. George determined the shrieking noise had to be silenced. On his way through the living room to the hall he picked up a brass candlestick and smashed the source of the noise, leaving plastic shards and smoke detector parts on the hall carpet. Finally, silence.

* * * * * * * * * * *

As he was drifting off to sleep, Steve was suddenly startled wide-awake by the distant sound of the chain saw. He sat up in bed, not sure of what disturbed him. Something made him uneasy. Something was wrong. He sat there listening in the dark. He looked at Linda, who was sound asleep. He noticed nothing but regular night sounds in the house: the clock ticked, the refrigerator hummed, the air conditioning made its usual muffled whistle. Still he was bothered. He pulled his loaded .357 Magnum from under the mattress, got up, and walked through the house. Steve checked on Andy, who was also sound asleep. He silently opened the door and stepped onto the front porch. No lights had been on so his eyes didn't have to adjust to the dark. He stood on the front porch, looking and listening for several moments. Seeing and hearing nothing unusual, he went back to bed. Sleep did not come easily. He replayed the day's events as he fingered the trigger under the pillow.

The two CIA agents systematically searched through Tom and Sharon's house, prowling through anything that might hold valuable items. They found many valuables but took nothing because the real treasure they sought eluded them – the gold medallion.

When they came up empty handed, J.T. felt compelled to confront his boss. "See, George, not everything can go according to plan all the time. Not every mission is successful, even when you're in on it."

"Shut up, J.T.! I get the point."

After checking his watch, George announced, "We've got to get out of here, or we'll be late for the rendezvous."

They stepped through the hole and back into the crawl space. As they made their way under the house, George quizzed J.T. on why he was dragging the chain saw behind him. J.T. explained that he didn't want to leave it behind to possibly be traced back to the point of purchase. The saw was not a CIA clean tool. George reluctantly agreed. After putting on the ski masks and starlight goggles, both men stepped into the back yard with the chain saw in tow. After another examination of the area, the two made a dash through the backyard, retracing their steps to the car. They stowed their equipment in the trunk and backed the car out to the road as slowly and quietly as they had come.

The two CIA professionals had attempted the mission, withdrawn and left the area unnoticed...or so they thought. Neither man saw the two shadowy figures, well camouflaged in the tall grass on a hill near the patch of woods, curiously watching and listening as the Mercedes disappeared from sight; and neither man noticed the faint glint of gold tightly clasped in one of the silvery hands.

There was very little traffic as they drove into town. About 15 minutes east of Indianapolis on I-74, the Mercedes found its exit. The service road that paralleled the interstate led to the back gate of the Indiana Air National Guard Station. JT turned off the lights and parked near the back fence.

The two agents got out of the car, opened the trunk, removed the plastic body bag, and moved toward the gate. J.T. used his picks on the lock in the gate chain. This lock was a stubborn one. It took almost two minutes to get it open. Nonetheless, the gate was opened enough to let them through and onto the parking area where many helicopters were tied down, including several Blackhawks, Apaches, and Hueys. The outlines of the dark green helicopters and the shadows of the buildings gave an ominous impression illuminated against the night. The landing pad marker poles with red lights on top added to an atmosphere of foreboding.

There was scarcely enough light to see by as J.T. and George carrying the black plastic bag between them, worked their way among the parked helicopters to a predetermined position at the edge of the landing pad. For the first time that night, J.T. had an uneasy feeling about being so exposed in unfamiliar territory. The four or five sentries he had expected to be guarding the helicopters were not on duty. And that's what bothered him. He couldn't see them. The reality was that there was only one guardsman on duty and he was allowed to sleep at night.

"Say, George?" J.T. whispered. "Too bad your pick up chopper has to meet us here instead of a cornfield where it would be safer!"

"Are you crazy?" George hissed. "That chopper pilot can find any single cornstalk in any cornfield in the whole state!"

The two men glared at each other. Their mutual disrespect was boiling over.

George continued, "My problem in planning this rendezvous was not if the pilot could find the pick up point but if you could get me to the right cornfield! I figured that there was only one place like this and you couldn't mess it up!"

J.T. seethed as he clenched his teeth. He thought, "I'll be so glad when this moron of a boss is on that chopper and out of my life."

At 4:30 J.T. impatiently looked at his watch and wondered where their contact was. Suddenly the scream of a turbine engine and the pounding throb of the rotor shook the otherwise soundless night. The Blackhawk barely cleared the nearby trees. It kicked up dirt and dust as it made a rapid descent to hover about a foot above the paved landing pad. The Blackhawk was on top of them before they were even aware that it was near. That, in itself, was unnerving. The pilot kept rpm high and the noise was deafening. A helmeted crewman jumped to the ground to assist J.T. with the plastic bag.

As George climbed to his seat and strapped himself in, he ordered J.T., "You find that medallion, you understand?"

The crewman and the bag followed immediately. As soon as the crewman was aboard, the helicopter shot skyward, brushed the tops of the trees, dived toward the grass on the other side, and departed into the darkness of night as quickly as it had come. Sacrificing speed and altitude for stealth, the Blackhawk could scarcely be heard. All this in less than one minute.

"I always did think army chopper pilots were crazy. Now I know they are." J.T. mouthed.

He ran to the car, not bothering to close the gate, jumped in, slammed the door, and sped down the service road. His spinning wheels threw gravel, dust and dirt as he went. By the time the guardsman on duty was startled awake by the noise and responded, the Blackhawk and the Mercedes were gone. All he found was a lot of dust blowing around on the landing pad. He was so sure that someone had stolen one of his helicopters that he notified the authorities immediately. But an equipment inventory count later in the morning would show that all the helicopters were there on the ground where they were supposed to be.

As dawn approached, the black Mercedes mingled into the traffic of Indianapolis.

CHAPTER 6

5:16 AM JUNE 15 CHURCH HILL, OHIO

The light filtering through the lace curtains of the cabin's bedroom awoke Sharon. For a few moments, she quietly listened to the sounds of morning at the lake. The sun, slightly below the horizon, cast a pastel glow over the entire area. A misty vapor hung low over the water in the lake. Where water met land the foggy vapor ended. Trees and grass were wet with dew. Birds began to flutter their wings and stretch. Their first morning songs announced a new day. Then a very gentle, occasional breeze began to rustle the leaves in the trees. Life began to stir. Soon the great ball of fire rose in the sky and the day began.

She looked at her sleeping husband, then got to her feet, slipped on her robe and went into the kitchen. She still felt the effects of the time she and Tom spent in the hammock the night before. "I'll let that be a lesson!" she thought as she reached for the coffee. "A bed is much gentler on the body than a hammock."

While the coffee was brewing, she watched through the window as bugs made ripples on the lake. The breeze and the warmth of the sun evaporated the mist and the lake area had come to life. She could see the other side of the lake. Fish leaped after bugs, causing big ripples in the water. "Breakfast at the fishpond," she thought.

She took the eggs, bacon, and a can of biscuits out of the refrigerator. While sipping on her first cup of coffee, Sharon started with bacon. When the oven warmed up she popped open a can of biscuits. Tom would wake up for all this. In the pantry she found a jar of her mom's homemade apple butter.

Sharon knew her husband all too well. The smells of bacon cooking and coffee brewing were more than enough to pull him from slumber. When Sharon sat on the edge of the bed, he only pretended to be asleep. He rolled over quickly and pulled her into bed with him. Sharon squealed with startled delight as covers and pillows went into disarray.

"No fooling around now," Sharon protested. "Breakfast will burn." A few seconds later the timer on the stove sounded. "Bread's done!" Sharon announced as she pulled away, got to her feet and hurried to the kitchen.

Tom rubbed his eyes, yawned, and stretched, then decided to go to the kitchen while breakfast was fresh off the stove. As Tom washed up, he too began to feel the results of the stay in the hammock.

When breakfast was finished, they pitched in to clean up. Sharon turned on the radio. The newscasters were well into the lead story about sporadic fighting between Israelis and Palestinians in Tel Aviv. The news anchor said that the Israeli army was on alert throughout the country to prevent further outbreaks.

"I'll go get dressed while you listen to the news. That stuff makes me nervous." Sharon said as she walked down the hall.

"Has all the Mideast gone nuts?" Tom asked himself.

The news anchor went on to say, "The hatred between the Palestinians and Israelis go back many years. But their most recent problems stem from the post WW II era when Britain and other nations mapped out the areas of the Mideast to be turned over to the Israelis and to the Palestinians. The UN approved the plan, and in 1948 their new nations were created. The Israelis accepted the terms of the agreement that established the Israeli state. The Palestinians refused the agreement that established the Palestinian state because they wanted to claim all the land, including the land of Israel. Their claim was denied by the U.N. The United States was the first to recognize the modern day state of Israel. Before the state of Israel was 24 hours old, the Arab world attacked. Israel fought back victoriously and remained a nation. The area designated to be the nation of Palestine was overrun and annexed by the nation of Jordan."

"Why then," Tom asked himself, "aren't the Palestinians angry at Jordan instead of Israel, since the only thing Israel did was successfully defend herself from neighboring invaders? When the Palestinians didn't claim the land designated for them, Jordan simply took it."

Sharon came back into the kitchen to find Tom standing at the kitchen sink with a half-cleaned plate in one hand and a soapy dishcloth in the other. He was not moving but was concentrating on the radio news. The news broadcast had shifted from the Mideast to China. As Tom listened intently to the broadcast, he thought, "Sounds like the Chinese are getting out their war wagons."

The newscaster said that the Chinese were going to back up their claim to possess land in the South China Sea area, which included island nations that had been independent for years, specifically Taiwan. The newscaster went on to say that China's brand new atomic nuclear destroyers along with their accompanying battle groups put to sea the previous week with little or no fanfare. The US Navy was tracking the nuclear destroyers and watching their activities with much interest.

"What's going on?" Sharon asked.

"I don't know," was Tom's reply. "It's like the whole world wants to square off and fight…the far east, near east, Europe, America, Africa…It's everywhere. One of these days some of these two bit potentates are going to push the wrong buttons at the wrong time and then it's going to be on for real."

"Tom, you're scaring me." Sharon said as she put her arms around him from behind.

Tom immediately regretted saying so much. He put the plate and cloth down, turned around and held her tight. "Not to worry. These crazy people have been rattling sabers at each other for years. It will blow over soon. Then start up somewhere else. It always does."

Tom didn't believe himself that it would blow over this time but he felt he had to say something to comfort Sharon. For some reason these news events sounded different… ominous, more deadly than usual.

He pondered the situation. From news accounts he had been reading, some of the weapons systems that China used came from technology stolen from the West. One editorial he read said that in some cases, weapons systems were sold to or given outright to China in return for special political favors. China, in turn, had seen to it that certain Islamic countries in the Persian Gulf area had their share of these weapons as well. The Chinese were more than willing to supply missiles and warheads for a missile-launching submarine sold to the Iranians by Russia to make Iran a nuclear force. In exchange, Iran promised to use its influence to help the Chinese secure oil exploration rights from among the Islamic nations.

Tom remembered a radio talk show host's conjecture that China would try to build an alliance with Islamic nations in order to quickly take over the world's biggest oil supply. Then it could hold the West and the rest of the world hostage. The host went on to say that neither China by itself, nor other Islamic nations by themselves, were strong enough to execute such a feat, but an alliance among those nations would be a formidable force.

The host reasoned that other things China had done seemed to point in that direction. China had secured berthing rights at both ends of the Panama Canal. That could allow the canal to be blocked at anytime. The Chinese, with a Mid-eastern alliance, could also block the Suez Canal.

The host seemed to be alarmed as he stated that the situation was worse than most people imagined. A communist Chinese shipping company called COSCO had secured rights to a nearby abandoned U.S. air force base. From these locations, the Chinese agents had smuggled weapons, drugs, and other contraband into the United States at will for years. The smuggled material was then offered for sale on the black market.

It seemed to Tom that many knew about these ventures, but no one did anything about it, not the government, not the police, not anyone. Maybe Sharon had a reason to be anxious.

Sharon noticed a somewhat worried look on Tom's face, exaggerated by the facial discoloration. She knew her husband well enough to know that he was at least a little concerned about the radio news, but she would appear to be comforted so he wouldn't worry about her. When the news switched to music the mood changed.

Tom picked up the portable radio and they walked out onto the covered front porch. Sharon's mom had her usual array of red geraniums in clay pots adorning the wide wooden rails. Conveniently, off in one corner of the porch was the old tin watering can that had been passed down through several generations. Sharon made a mental note to use it to water the flowers before they left. They listened to the sweet sounds of stringed instrumental music coming from the radio, occasionally picking up a whiff of the honeysuckle that twined its way around the rails of the fence that led to the dock.

They gazed at the sunlight sparkling on the lake and watched a dragonfly gliding across the water's surface trolling for victims. Propelled by its four wings it expertly snatched mosquitoes, gnats, and other various insect pests.

"Seems to me the only ones having any luck today are the dragonflies. The fish apparently aren't very hungry. They're not taking anyone's bait," Sharon remarked as she watched a couple of fishermen from other cabins around the edges of the lake.

"Why bother to even try our luck this morning?" Tom said to Sharon. "Let's go for a walk and see how things have changed around here, if they have at all."

One thing that hadn't changed was the squirrel wheel. It was always out of corn. Tom went to the back porch to get an ear of dried corn from the storage container. He placed it on the spike at the outside edge of the wheel. The bait was set. Sharon remembered many hours sitting in her dad's lap laughing as they watched the squirrels perform their antics as they chased after the ear of corn, going round and round on the wheel.

They walked hand in hand down the well-worn path that led through the field and to the woods behind the cabin. The rich cedar aroma from the bushes at the edge of the porch mixed with the fragrance of the abundant colorful assortment of wildflowers that grew profusely in the field. Bees were busily gathering nectar from nature's smorgasbord. Sharon remembered that as a small child, she tried to catch rabbits and butterflies in this same field. They were always too quick.

As Sharon and Tom approached the woods, she recalled that when she was a little girl and the cabin was new she played among these same trees. As they ambled through the woods Sharon allowed pleasant childhood memories to surface. Memories of the many games of make-believe she played among the trees. One tree in particular stood out in Sharon's mind—— the climbing tree. From her perch in this tree she imagined the stories of Sherwood Forest with Robin Hood and his merry men engaged in their adventurous deeds. In her mind she could hear horses galloping through the woods and the shouts of the merry men echoing through the trees. From this same perch she could look out over the lake and envision herself to be in the crow's nest high on the mast of a pirate's ship as she sailed the high seas.

Many other pleasant memories were not imaginary. Sharon remembered when her dad would come to the foot of the tree and pretend he didn't know where she was and call out to her as if she were lost. Only when she giggled would he look up into the tree and "discover" his daughter on her perch. She would gleefully climb down and into her father's waiting arms. "So, where have you been today?" he would ask. "Were you hiding from the Sheriff of Nottingham or were you sounding the alarm for the pirates on your ship?"

Oh, how she cherished the memories of her childhood – such warm and happy memories. These were the times when Sharon longed in vain for a child of her own- children with which she could make similar memories. That empty feeling of barrenness surfaced often.

Pleasant memories came crashing to an end when she saw the weathered boards of an unfinished tree house high in a tree just ahead — the climbing tree. Sharon felt an icy coldness sweep over her as she remembered the day she fell. Her father had started her tree house and just a few boards were in place. Her fall was only from the bottom limb and she was left only slightly shaken. She could think of no reason why she felt the way she did. She had always enjoyed the tree, but since that day the tree seemed evil and menacing. She never climbed the tree again.

Tom was concerned by her sudden change in mood but thought

it best not to ask any questions. He too had felt an unpleasant cold-ness as they approached the tree. They continued on to the stream that fed the lake. They took off their shoes and waded in the cool, refreshing water, all the while watching for the rainbow trout they knew were there.

As it neared mid-afternoon, they drifted back to the cabin. Hunger pangs drove them straight to the kitchen. "Does your face hurt at all?" Sharon asked as she sipped the cold glass of iced tea.

"Not at all!" Tom replied. "Do I look really bad? I've deliber-ately not looked in a mirror for awhile."

"Let's just put it this way, I'm glad we're not having lunch at a fancy restaurant right now."

When they finished their snack, Tom busied himself gathering the fishing equipment while Sharon went to the front porch. She noticed that some corn was gone from the squirrel wheel. "Guess we missed a good show," she said aloud. The screen door slammed with a bang as Tom came through with an armload of fishing rods and tackle boxes. He was barely hanging on to his load, grabbing falling things as he walked. His hat filled with fishing hooks and flies sat atop the entire mess. He had raided the worm farm for some bait. "If you'll get the lounge chairs and radio and bring them down to the lake, we'll be ready to catch our supper. Oh, bring the camera too."

"You're gonna take pictures of all the fish you haul out of the lake, are you?" Sharon quipped. "Do you have enough film?"

"You wait and see," said Tom. "This is gonna be good."

With lounge chairs set up, "oldies" music playing, hooks baited and in the water, the couple settled in for an afternoon's fishing. That was the kind of fishing they liked to do, sit in a chair, half asleep, and watch the float to see if a fish hit bait. If either of them caught a fish, very good. If not, that too was good. It was a definite win-win situa-tion. It was really the drifting off into a nap that made this endeavor worthwhile in Tom's estimation. Tom joked to Sharon, "It's not called fishing anymore; it's called looking at the water."

At the very far end of the lake where there were two cabins, an older man and woman were also lounging while they fished.

"Looks like the Pritchards are still enjoying their retirement in seclusion," Sharon commented as she waved hello.

"You know, I believe they were sitting in that same spot when we were here five years ago," Tom remarked as he returned their wave.

Off to the left and about one fourth of the way around the lake was a solitary man who had apparently come to do some serious fishing. He was standing near the water and really working his line. "Must be staying in the rental cabin beside the Pritchards," Sharon said.

Tom sat up with a start. Sharon jumped at his sudden move.

"Look at the size of the fish he caught!" Tom pointed to the man. "That fish is huge! Watch the lines, honey; I'm going to take a picture of him."

After capturing the moment on film, Tom announced to Sharon that he would take a picture of them before they caught their big fish.

"Sort of a before and after thing?" Sharon laughed. "You really expect to make the big catch, do you? Together the two of us haven't caught ten fish in seventeen years of marriage."

Undaunted, Tom continued a little way up the bank to a weathered wooden post where he could place the camera. He aimed, focused, and set the camera timer so that a picture could be taken just the way he wanted it. Out of the corner of his eye, he saw the man pull in another big fish.

"What's he got going for himself?" Sharon asked Tom.

"Whatever it is, it's good!" came the reply.

Tom released the timer and hurried back down the slope toward his chair. He estimated that by the time he got to his seat, he would have six seconds to spare. The time would allow for a silly pose. As Tom rounded the corner of his chair, his foot slipped on the grass and he went flying, landing in the water on his back. The splash was big enough to get the attention of the Pritchards at the far end of the lake. They laughed and the lone man grinned. Tom stood up in waist deep water. Click. The camera captured the moment for posterity. The great fisherman in action, dripping wet, hair pasted to his head, smeared with mud. For a few seconds Sharon just sat with her hands over her mouth, wondering if he were hurt. Tom turned around and wiped the water out of his eyes. Sharon burst out in laughter. She was overjoyed at the prospect of putting this picture in the album.

"I guess the fishing won't be good in this spot for a while," Tom said as he wrung out his shirt. "I'll go change clothes."

"OK. I'll fix the poles and move to another spot. The fish will definitely be spooked here for a while," Sharon laughed as she gathered up their things. "These unplanned dives into the water are getting to be a habit," she thought as she remembered his story of a dive into the water-filled ditch two nights earlier.

Sharon moved everything to another shady spot closer to the lone fisherman. All Tom had to do was sit in his chair and get ready to catch the big one. "What a joke," Sharon laughed to herself. Neither she nor Tom had ever caught a big one, but then they really hadn't tried very hard either.

Sharon watched as the man pulled in yet another large fish. "Wow," she thought, "I'd better get ready. A fish that big could pull the poles into the water fast."

She grabbed her pole and reached over to secure Tom's.

Shortly Tom returned wearing fresh clothes. He could see that the fisherman had worked his way closer to their spot. He noticed Sharon's tight grip on the two poles and ribbed her with, "Are the poles going to run away?"

"Yes," she replied, "if fish as big as those take the bait." Tom looked over to see the fisherman pull in yet another large fish.

"Has that guy put the third fish on his stringer?"

"No" Sharon replied. "That's number five! Wait a minute and you'll see."

When the man pulled the stringer out of the water, Tom could count the fish. They were five of the biggest fish Tom had ever seen. The fisherman carried the stringer a little closer to where they were sitting and began fishing again.

"What are you using for bait?' Tom called out.

"Just bread pieces," the man replied. "It seems to work out very well."

"I'll say it does. We're using worms, but I think we'll change to bread."

Sharon went into the cabin to get bread. While she was gone, the master fisherman pulled in another fish.

"I can't believe that! I didn't know there were fish that big in this lake."

"The fishing is excellent here," the man said.

"It is for some people. We haven't had a single nibble, but then again you haven't been swimming and fishing in the same spot like we have." Both men laughed.

Sharon brought bread and a pitcher of cold lemonade. And, anticipating the visit, she had also brought three glasses.

"Care for some lemonade?" she called to the man.

"Love some. I'll be there in just a minute."

It appeared to Tom that the man was having some trouble handling his load of fish, rod and tackle box, so Tom walked around the edge of the lake to help him move his things over. Tom took the fishing pole and tackle box from the man, who began lifting his stringer of fish from the water. For the first time since coming to the lake, Tom became self-conscious about his discolored face and wondered if the man would notice. Up close this man looked strangely familiar. In his heart, Tom felt that their paths had crossed before. But where?

CHAPTER 7

━══━

A ctivity began simply enough around the old government-owned building in suburban Fairfax, Virginia. A windowless green van with U.S. Army stenciled on the front doors backed up to the basement entrance. Two men carried a large black bag from the van into the building. They locked the door to the basement then drove away. To the casual observer, these activities were not out of the ordinary and not worthy of attention.

A short while later, two black Mercedes sedans parked at the same basement entrance. From one car stepped the driver, dressed in a dark suit, and three other men wearing pale green medical scrubs. Each of the three carried a black duffel bag. Inside the bags was specialized examination equipment. In the second Mercedes were three dark-suited men. Each man entered the building through the basement door.

No one came in or out until late in the afternoon when one of the dark suited men came out to meet another olive drab van, this one loaded with uniformed and armed Army MPs. The soldiers were assigned guard duty at each exterior door around the building.

As the day wore on, the area around the building became a beehive of activity as limousines came and went, allowing their government passengers time to rendezvous within. IDs were checked and signatures were required from each person before entrance was allowed into the building.

The CIA operative known as George had secured a team of

pathologists from the government staff pool. They conducted an autopsy of sorts on the specimen George had transported from Indianapolis.

During the autopsy a startling discovery was made. Immediately security went from non-existent to a level of national importance requiring top secret security clearance. Safety measures would remain in place for as long as the contents of the plastic bag were on the premises. Each person present was sworn to secrecy.

Night came, and with it, the changing of the guard.

CHAPTER 8

A s the accomplished fisherman pulled the overloaded stringer from the water, Tom saw seven of the finest bass ever taken from the lake. "That's a nice load of fish," Tom said, eyeing the catch.

"They're heavy, too," the man said. "I always turn them loose or give them away. Would you care to take them?"

"Sure, I'd be happy to take them."

The two men walked the short distance to the shaded area where Sharon was sitting in a lawn chair.

Tom laid down the items he volunteered to carry.

"I'm Tom Alexander and this is my wife Sharon."

"Thanks for your help; I'm Charles Levi. Pleased to meet you."

Tom observed that Charles had the appearance and speech of a distinguished and well-educated man. He guessed him to be around 55 years of age. He was about six one, 210 pounds, with an athletic build and ramrod straight posture. His hair was salt and pepper, thick, and well groomed. His beard was neatly trimmed, mostly gray, and came to a small point at the tip of his chin. Charles' tan added to his distinction. His voice was clear and seemed to come from deep within his being. He was wearing fishing boots and a khaki fishing vest over a pair of dark gray coveralls. Instead of a watch he wore a striking and unusual gold wristband with a single gemstone. It occurred to Tom that Charles could be an overpowering presence if he chose to be.

"Do you come here often?" Charles asked.

"Well, not really. We haven't been here in five years. The cabin belongs to Sharon's parents. We've always had an open invitation but we haven't been able to take advantage of it as often as we'd like. This time we're just spending a few days."

Tom complimented Sharon on the lemonade. She had made it double strong, just the way he liked it.

"Thank you," Sharon replied. "Do you like it Mr. Levi? Not everyone likes it that strong."

"Yes, this is perfect in my opinion, but please call me Charles. Don't stand on formalities just for me, OK?"

"Charles, what brings you to this part of the country?" Tom asked.

"Well," Charles said. "Normally I stay up north but I'm on my way south and was advised to stop here for the fishing."

The three walked to the old battered picnic table in the shade at the edge of the lake and continued their conversation as they cleaned and dressed the fish. They decided that since they were so big the fish could be handled, packaged, and cooked better if they were cut into quarters.

Sharon put the pieces of fish into plastic bags and took them to the refrigerator while Tom and Charles quartered them. As the three finished up their work on the fish Charles asked Sharon about their jobs.

"I teach high school English and Tom's a journalist and photographer. Although you would never know it from the stunt he pulled a little while ago. I can't wait to show off that picture!" They all laughed, remembering Tom's flop in the lake and the click of the camera.

"What do you do, Charles?"

"I work for an organization that you might call a think tank. We gather information about many things to evaluate and compile for research and publication. We're especially interested in the unusual events that happen to ordinary people — their endeavors, adventures, accomplishments, failures, and many other aspects of the human experience. These things are of special interest to us. We compile and use all this information to help people overcome the hardships and challenges of life and try to help them become successful. There are some very unique stories out there."

"I couldn't agree more," Tom said. "I experienced one of those unusual events a few days ago myself." Tom felt very relaxed talking to Charles. It was as if he were speaking to an old friend. He couldn't shake that sense of familiarity. Tom began telling his story one more time. He then remembered the newspaper in the car and decided to let Charles read the article. "Come on up to the car. I have a newspaper article complete with pictures. You can read the story for yourself."

As Tom took the newspaper from the trunk, Charles complimented him on the condition of the car.

"Thanks," Tom said "but I can't take all the credit. A lot of hard work went into restoring this beauty."

Tom handed the newspaper to Charles. As Charles read the article, Tom looked out over the lake. He noticed there were pockets of fishermen all around the lake. Yet during his observation he didn't see anyone pull in a fish.

"Very unusual story," Charles said when he finished reading. "Is this the only time anything like this has ever happened to you?"

"Yes," Tom replied, "The article says that my encounter was a near miss lightning strike, but it wasn't!"

"Is that so?" Charles questioned.

"Yes, I've only used reference to lightning strike as an oversimplified explanation. I know for a fact this wasn't even close to a lightning strike, but I have no idea what it really was."

Tom and Charles discussed the details of his encounter, especially the puzzling details of seeing figures and shapes move about inside the brightly lit area of the meadow. Those things were not mentioned in the newspaper article. Charles seemed very interested. Tom had told only Sharon and very few others about that. For some unknown reason he felt a compulsion to tell this man the whole story. Charles listened intently and seldom interrupted.

"I've heard about things like this. Let's talk more a little later. Right now, tell me more about your Thunderbird," Charles said as he deliberately changed the subject.

"O.K.," Tom said. Then, with typical classic car owner pride, he continued, "It took over two years to get this baby into mint condition. It was completely torn down and rebuilt from the ground up."

"It looks like it just came out of the showroom," Charles said.

"That was the goal," replied Tom with a big smile. "It runs better than a new one."

Tom unlocked the driver's door and asked Charles. "Do you want to take her for a spin?" Tom had no idea why he was turning his "baby" over to a stranger. He just felt the need to make the offer.

"Sure! That would be great!" Charles replied quickly.

Tom unlocked the passenger door, pulled the vinyl top down and called to Sharon, "Hey, honey, we're going for a joy ride."

Sharon knew that Tom was always looking for someone to take for a joy ride. He would find any excuse he could to drive the T-bird anywhere. Sharon smiled because she knew that the joy ride would take them over Roller Coaster Hills, an attraction for local speedsters. "He's just a big kid with his favorite toy," she thought. "I'll have a snack ready when you get back," she called out.

"Sounds great!" Charles answered back.

"Just jump in and adjust the seat to suit you," Tom encouraged Charles.

Charles pushed the seat all the way back. It fit exactly. "Good thing I'm not an inch taller," Charles said, "or this might not work."

Tom grinned and waited for Charles to start the engine. He liked to see the faces of people when they heard the engine for the first time. Charles turned the key. The engine leaped to life with a loud but deep, mellow roar, then settled to its normal idling chug, the mark of a high compression, high performance engine. There was that look, the widening of the eyes, the cocking of the head to get the best sound, the smile and stare at the instrument panel as the engine purred. Tom could tell when people who really appreciate mechanical things heard his car. They loved it. Charles was no exception. Tom was pleased. He smiled.

"What do you think?" Tom asked, setting the bait for a compliment.

"What a rich sound!" Charles said. "What's under the hood? That's not an original engine."

"No, it's not! It's a 1966 Ford 390 engine. It has dual 500 CFM low profile four-barrel carburetors."

"Wow! I didn't think it was a factory engine. That's a power-house!"

"Well, it's the biggest engine we could get in there and still shut the hood."

"So, you made it a 'snoozer." Charles said deliberately misusing the term to inject a bit of humor.

Tom laughed out loud. "No, no, it's a 'sleeper!'"

"Ah, yes, a 'sleeper!'" Charles chuckled. "Let's see how she runs."

"Let her rip!" Tom replied.

A smooth, mellow tone trailed off in the distance as Sharon watched them go toward the highway. Sharon was puzzled that Tom would allow someone he'd just met drive his car. But Charles some-how evoked a feeling of friendship and trust.

Charles turned south onto the two-lane highway. It stretched for several miles over rolling hills and around gentle curves. He gradu-ally picked up speed as he became accustomed to the feel of the car. Sailing along at just under the speed limit, Charles noticed that the steering was very responsive to his touch. He could feel the forces of acceleration and the pull of the curves as they went around them. He had never driven a car that handled so precisely.

"Out here in the country you can open her up some. Trust me. Run the speed up to 67 miles an hour and hold it there," Tom told Charles, knowing Roller Coaster Hills were dead ahead.

Charles pushed on the accelerator and felt the car surge forward. He watched the speedometer needle climb to 67 and kept it there. At 67 mph the T-bird rose to about a foot off the ground at the crest of the first hill. It had enough speed to make it sail through the air for about 100 feet. Because the trajectory of the car and the curvature of the hill were so much alike the car was never more than a foot off the ground. The engine picked up rpm and the rear wheels began to spin much faster. When the car came in contact with the road again the rear wheels barked a squeal as the tires grabbed the asphalt. The car settled firmly on the pavement before they got to the valley between the first and second hills. Once in the low point of the valley, the G-forces began to build rapidly as the car started its ascent up the next hill. For an instant in the valley, the car and its riders weighed twice their normal weight. At the crest of the second hill the roller coaster ride continued. For the next two miles they crossed smaller hills. As the car came to the top of the little hills they could feel the wheels almost leave the ground for a split second. The tug of their bodies on the lap belts told them that they were just at the limit of speed for this road. Charles let off the accelerator and looked at Tom who was grinning. Roller Coaster Hills lived up to its name. Tom had discovered the secret of the 67 mph speed years ago; not a mile slower, not a mile faster. It thrilled him to take the uninitiated for a ride. Most people enjoyed the way the car handled, but Charles seemed exceptionally impressed. He related every sensation he felt in descriptive detail. Tom usually enjoyed the joy ride as much as his guests but Charles bubbled over with excitement as if he were a sixteen year old with his hands on the wheel for the first time. Reluctantly Charles slowed back to the speed limit before they entered a steep curve. He turned the car around at a side road and headed back toward the lake, enthusiastically recounting the details of Roller Coaster Hills.

While riding back, Tom told Charles the history of how he, Sharon, and Jim had restored the car inside and out. He related how Sharon had worked wonders reconditioning the inside, complete with rolled and pleated upholstery, as he and Jim worked on the mechanics of the car. Tom expounded on particulars of the '66 Ford 390 engine and described the C6 speed shift transmission with the 9-inch Positrac rear end. Tom's listener was genuinely impressed.

Charles parked the car near the front porch. They got out, pulled up the vinyl top, latched it securely in place, rolled up the windows and locked the doors. The two men's smiles projected their sheer joy and pleasure as each admired the T-bird.

"Yes! She's a 'sleeper' alright!" Charles confirmed.

As they walked toward the porch, they heard Sharon call out.

"Do you guys hear this?" Sharon said as she turned the radio louder. The radio news reported that the fighting in Jerusalem had spread to other Israeli cities. Small arms clashes were taking place all over Israel. Spurred by rhetoric from Iran, Islamic nations all around the Mideast were threatening Israel with war if it did not stop the hard line activities at the Wailing Wall. Hard line Jewish fundamentalists were demanding their right to build their temple on Temple Mount now that they had a coalition government with the political will to back the idea. The hard liners contended that they would be able to build their temple and leave the two existing Islamic Holy places intact in the Temple's outer court, which had been traditionally set aside for Gentiles. The Jewish fundamentalists also contended that Temple Mount could be used by all for peaceful worship. The Islamic factions would have none of it, the commentator reported. They demanded that the Jews and the Israeli government discard the idea in order to save the Mideast from unprecedented, bloody war. Iranian-supported Palestinians swore to call down "fire from heaven" on the idea of a Jewish temple.

The whole newscast was about that one story. The situation in the Mid-east was becoming more and more serious.

"Looks like those people are throwing gas on the fire again," Tom said as he and Charles made their way to the cabin.

"Indeed it does," said Charles as he climbed the steps that led to the porch.

"Why are those people always fighting?" asked Sharon as she filled three mugs with hot coffee and set a tray of snacks on the glass-topped wicker table.

"Well," Charles said thoughtfully as he sipped the steaming cup of coffee, "I think I can shed some light on the subject. That just happens to be in my area of expertise. Our group has done exhaustive research on matters concerning the Mideast. The news media is not reporting the whole story. The real truth is that the complaint the Moslems have against the Israelis has little to do with what the Jews are doing at the Wailing Wall and Temple Mount. Students of Islam are taught almost nothing about Jewish traditions concerning that particular site. The average student of Islam can't understand why the Israelis, and Jews in particular, have any claim at all to Temple Mount. The officials of Islam are the people who are stirring up the trouble and they are being goaded by outside forces."

"Do you think this could break out into war?" Tom asked.

"There's always that possibility," said Charles. "These hatreds run so deep that all it takes is a small spark to start a big fire. The

Mideast is a tinderbox. Since the Iran and Iraq war Iran has been one of the very few countries that has not had a drain on its military strength because of war. Iran has been able to build its defenses mainly by the purchase of sophisticated weapons from the former Soviet Union, China and North Korea. As time has passed, Iran has become stronger and stronger. Iran is Persian. It is not an Arab country, but its strong ties through Islamic faith have projected its influence into the Arab world."

Charles went on to explain that his group knew in fact that there are Israelis who are preparing to build the third temple on Temple Mount. "The Islamic fundamentalists don't like it at all."

"Why not?" Sharon asked. "What do they care if the Israelis build a temple there?"

"It's their holy site. The followers of Islam believe that Mohammed ascended into heaven from the place where the Dome of the Rock mosque stands. They say that a temple can't be built as long as the mosque stands in that place."

"Oh," Sharon replied. "I think I'm beginning to get the picture."

"And a bloody picture at that," added Tom. "Charles, what are you talking about, what kind of preparations are they making for building the temple?"

Charles thought for a few moments, and then said, "Some Israelis have already carved the cornerstone and are collecting material suitable for temple construction."

"I think I remember from Sunday school days the temple being covered with gold," said Tom.

Charles answered, "Yes. There was a lot of gold used in that temple. Most of the cedar wood was covered with gold."

"Do the present day Israelis have gold available to put into that temple?"

"They do now!" Charles answered emphatically. "Recently discovered in Switzerland is at least 30 tons of gold, including dental gold and jewelry, taken from the death camps in Germany. You see," he went on, "it seems that rather than being neutral in World War II, the Swiss were the Nazis' bankers. The gold that they have acknowledged as belonging to the Jews may be only a fraction of what is really there. There are still unopened vaults in the Swiss banks."

"So they might find more gold in the vaults?" Sharon mused. "Charles, you said other preparations are being made for the temple. Like what?"

Charles replied. "Well, they're gathering linen articles for making seamless garments for the priests. You know, the Navajo Indians showed the Israelis how to weave a seamless garment."

"Navajos? What do the Navajos have to do with the Israelis?" asked Sharon.

"During their many years of captivity, the Israelis lost their identity as a people. They lost some of their customs and traditions as well, including their knowledge of weaving seamless garments. The Navajos have preserved in their traditions the pattern for weaving these kinds of garments. The Israelis simply programmed the pattern into a computer. Now machinery does the weaving. Others have fabricated many items to be used in the temple. They're keeping all these things in storage until the time comes for their use."

"When will that time be?" Sharon asked wondering how this man could be so well-informed. She was unaware that for the past several hours Charles had intentionally directed the conversation.

Charles seemed lost in thought while he pondered Sharon's question, taking more time than his listeners thought he should for such a simple question. Dusk had settled in and the last vestiges of light filtered through the trees. The gentle hint of wood smoke with the sweet smell of hardwood tinted the air from campfires burning on the far side of the lake. Sharon lit the torch lights on either side of the porch. Fireflies flickered above the darkened lawn.

"'Next year in Jerusalem!' is the cry of those who long for the rebuilding of the temple. It is the refrain the Jews that were scattered to other nations have used for centuries to encourage one another concerning the rebuilding of the Temple." Charles replied. "Every year on the Day of Atonement, the cornerstone for the temple is presented to the Israeli government and permission asked for the cornerstone to be placed on Temple Mount. Every year permission is denied. One day permission will be granted. So, there is not an exact answer to your question at this time. The issue is very complex, but the temple will be built. The temple and everything in it must be sanctified."

"How will that be done?"

"By using the ashes from a sacrificial red heifer."

"You mean they still do sacrifices?" Sharon asked.

"Not now, but the time will come when sacrifices will begin again for a short time. Then they will be stopped again."

"Tell us about this red heifer and why it's so important," said Sharon.

Charles explained, "They have at least one red heifer now that meets specifications for the sanctifying sacrifice. The strange part of this is the calf was born to a black and white cow and reddish-brown and white bull. Religious officials have examined the calf with magnifying glasses. They are trying to find even one hair that isn't colored red. They can't find one. This calf is being well taken care of and is under guard somewhere in Israel."

"How do they use this calf in a sacrifice?"

"The ashes of the red heifer are mixed with water and used in a sanctifying ceremony to purify the temple and its contents. The ashes of today's red heifer must be mixed with the original sacrificial ashes to complete the sacrament." Charles continued, "You see, since the people of ancient Israel fled from Egypt, nine red heifers have been offered for sacrifice. The ashes of the successive heifers have been mixed with the previous ones so that there is always a trace of the first red heifer that dates back to the time of Moses. The original sacrificial ashes have been lost until now. The hiding place has been recently discovered. The Islamic officials fully understand the impact of this find."

"What do you mean? What's the impact of the find? If they've found the ancient ashes, then why don't they go ahead with their plans?" Tom questioned, amazed at Charles' depth of knowledge.

Charles studied the question thoughtfully for a few moments. One torch light sputtered, blending with other sounds as night creatures crept and crawled around in the edges of the darkness as if reluctant to enter the torches' light.

He replied in a subdued and serious tone, "Today Jews have no place to worship on Temple Mount because Muslims are in possession. You can only imagine the reaction in the Islamic world if they suspected even one Jew removed a single stone from the mosque in an effort to build the temple. There would be a war the likes of which the world has never seen."

"So that's what you meant by a small spark starting a big fire."

"Yes. The Islamic religious leaders are initiating guerilla-style firefights all over Israel. They're trying to get their Islamic sympathizers to exterminate the nation of Israel. The descendents of Isaac and Ishmael have been fighting each other for thousands of years, beginning when Israelis and Palestinians were called Israelites and Philistines. They will never be able to get along."

Tom paused and reflected on all that Charles had said. "The trouble that the world is experiencing today didn't just happen today. It has been thousands of years in the making. I've been reading. I follow the news, too."

Campfires were slowly dying away. Glowing embers had replaced dancing flames. All the cabins that circled the lake were now dark. The lack of fireflies and absence of bug noises prompted Charles to say, "It's getting so late even the bugs have gone to bed."

"Come on over tomorrow," Sharon invited, "and Tom will treat you to a real fish fry...say around 6?"

With this invitation, Charles said his goodnight and walked down the path at the edge of the lake.

"Did you notice?" Sharon asked. "He never once mentioned your face."

CHAPTER 9

Raindrops splattered on the kitchen windowsill. Heavy dark clouds filtered the once rich sunlit colors into an uninviting gray hue.

"What's the matter, honey?" Tom asked as he walked into the kitchen and saw the expression on Sharon's face.

"Listen to this! It's more of the news we heard yesterday."

The newscaster described the intermittent fighting in Israel and gave more information about the Chinese nuclear destroyer fleet that was displaying an offensive stance toward Taiwan. He went on to add to the already depressing news by reporting unusual troop movements in Iraq, Egypt, Syria, and Libya. The newscaster described the most alarming part of the news; the Iranians had accepted delivery of a Russian made submarine. Satellites and the U.S. Navy's Orion anti-submarine aircraft had tracked the submarine into the Iranian port. U.S. Navy officials could identify the submarine by her Bow number, 504. It was being armed with Chinese-made nuclear medium range missiles. Pentagon officials had notified the President and ranking members of Congress that an extremely dangerous situation was beginning to develop. China had openly threatened to invade Taiwan and the Iranians threatened to annihilate Israel.

"Sometimes you don't know whether to believe these newscasters or not," Tom said as he turned the radio off. He could see that Sharon was becoming upset.

By mid-morning the rain had slowed to a fine mist and the sun peeked through the scattered puffy clouds. By late afternoon the rain had stopped and clouds had moved away, leaving a crystal clear, freshly washed sky behind. The bright sunshine lifted their spirits from the doldrums of the dismal morning and the radio news.

Tom and Sharon gathered all the supplies they would need for the fish fry and took them to the picnic tables near the back porch to await Charles' arrival. They had spent the better part of the day talking about their visitor from the night before. Charles had caused them to think about things they had never considered. They found themselves eagerly awaiting his visit that evening. At precisely the appointed time, Tom and Sharon heard Charles whistling as he walked up the trail toward their cabin.

"Are you ready for the best fried fish you've ever tasted?" Tom called out.

"I've been ready for good fried fish ever since you mentioned it last night," came the reply.

Sharon began laying out the chilled vegetables for the salad. "Would you allow me to do that job?" Charles said.

"I was just about to start chopping," Sharon said, "but help yourself."

Charles took the sharp knife and began to slice and dice the vegetables, humming a lively tune while he worked.

Sharon commented that the tune sounded familiar to her so Charles added the words to the amusing little song and they all laughed. He sang several more songs that were equally entertaining and, having learned that Tom and Sharon liked 'oldies' songs, he chose a couple of ballads from the 50's and 60's that were on the serious side. One was the story of a boy and his dog. The other ballad he sang was about a young man riding his horse through a blinding snowstorm to reach his sweetheart's house.

Charles was quite the balladeer. His full baritone voice had a rich tone that resonated across the water. The words of the last two ballads expressed a heartfelt message that brought tears to Sharon's eyes. He then announced he would sing his favorite. Charles' voice was larger than life. The area around the picnic table seemed transformed into a stage at a large amphitheater. His dramatic voice projected itself throughout the area of the lake. The echo from the trees became his accompaniment as creation joined his performance. The song told the story of the Savior's grace and His extreme sacrifice. When Charles finished singing, a stirring breeze caused the leaves to seem to cheer, and then there was silence at the table. Not only Charles' spectacular voice, but also the powerful message of the music stirred their souls and left them speechless.

Tom had listened in amazement, pondering, as he somehow sensed familiarity in Charles' voice. The tender moment was interrupted by sounds from across the lake. All three turned to see the Pritchards standing by the lakeshore clapping their approval — a standing ovation! Charles waved and did an exaggerated stage bow to acknowledge their appreciation. He turned to Tom and Sharon to say that it always pleased him to see people happy to hear the story of the Redeemer. Through her tears Sharon said that the last one was the most beautiful love song she had ever heard. For a moment she studied Charles thoughtfully. He seemed so familiar to her...but why?

"Well," Tom spoke up, regaining his composure, "Are you ready for my dad's famous recipe for fried fish?"

"I am," Charles replied.

Sharon jabbed at Tom with, "You're going to tell your dad's fish cooking story again, aren't you?"

"You gotta tell the story to cook the fish you know," was Tom's standard reply.

Tom explained that every time his dad cooked fish, he had to tell the whole story of how best to deep fry fish, from putting the ingredients together to make the batter all the way through to placing the fish on the plates.

Sharon quipped, "Apples don't fall far from the tree. He tells the same story his dad does, even if it's just with me. Charles, one time, on this very spot he was in the back yard by himself. I heard him from the kitchen tell the whole story without a soul in sight."

So the ritual began; Tom got out two deep iron skillets and filled them halfway with corn oil and placed them over the already hot charcoal. While the oil heated, he explained the secret of the batter. Then he carefully rolled the cleaned and scaled fish quarters into the batter and stacked them on a platter, ready to be dropped into the oil. He explained to Charles that everything: the ingredients in the batter, the type of cooking oil, the temperature of the charcoal, the deep black iron skillets, all had unique contributions to the flavor of the fish, but the most important one was the onion.

As the quarters of battered fish were carefully dropped into the hot oil, a bubbling, boiling sound indicated that the temperature was just right. When the skillet was full of fish, a golf ball sized onion was dropped in. It sank immediately to the bottom. Tom was quick to relate his dad's observation that it was at this point one could forget about the fish and concentrate on the onion. When the onion bobbed to the top of the boiling oil, the fish were cooked to absolute perfection.

"Not only is the onion a thermometer to tell when the fish is done," Tom explained, "but it adds that onion flavor to the fish."

The other boiling skillet contained hushpuppies made from Sharon's special recipe. Sharon arranged the plates, silverware and napkins while Tom cooked. She went into the kitchen to get the tea and a bucket of ice. Just on cue, everything was ready. The steaming morsels were laid on the plates and the feast began.

"Tom, you're right," Charles said. "Your dad's recipe for deep fried fish is just about the best I've ever experienced. My diet normally consists of less substantial stuff but this is surely one of the best meals I've had in a good while."

Dinner conversation was light. Sharon talked about how much she enjoyed teaching, and Tom spoke about some of the projects he was working on at the paper. As the dying charcoal embers spread their aroma through the air, they listened. The frogs at the edge of the lake began their evening chorus, and the crickets added their serenade. The sun dipped lower in the sky and a pinkish glow was deepening on the horizon. A lone boat drifted at its moorings beside the dock. For a moment there was silence at the table, each person lost in thought.

Charles said, "You know, I've been thinking about your article and what you told me yesterday concerning your experience in the meadow."

"Funny you should mention that—I was just thinking about the very same thing," replied Tom.

"Tell me more about what happened that night."

"Well, most of what I remember was just quick glimpses. It's hard to explain. It all happened so fast. If you could just picture in your mind a movie screen suspended in mid air just above the ground with a background of glowing light. Within this glowing light there were other more intensely lighted undefined shapes moving about. It was difficult to look at it for more than a few seconds. The brightness of the light caused the images and details within to be indistinct and blurred. A brilliant, focused beam of light exploded from one of those undefined shapes. My neighbor said he saw two figures running away from the area and into the woods. I didn't see them, but the next day I did see footprints in the grass that could have been made by those two figures. I saw one shadowy figure run from the meadow back into the brightly-lit area just as if it were running into an open door."

Charles said, "From time to time there is evidence that there are windows in the dimensions of time and space, similar to what you have described. That may sound fantastic but it is documented from many different places. Even the Bible records such scenes."

"You mean like science fiction?" Sharon asked.

"Yes, science, but not fiction," Charles answered. "There is a story of the prophet Elisha in the Bible that describes a scene similar to Tom's meadow experience. Elisha prayed that his servant would be allowed to see the horses and chariots of fire from the spiritual realm. His prayer request was answered. The servant was allowed to see. There are many other instances such as this recorded in the Bible that go back for thousands of years. If there are events such as those described in the Bible, then why not similar events today? Do the descriptions of these two events, Elisha's and yours, sound similar?"

"Yes, now that you point it out. They really do!"

"You see," Charles went on, "The Creator is in control of the entire universe. It is difficult for people to understand all of its workings. There are many things that happen that are absolutely unexplainable because people don't have the ability to understand. It would be like trying to explain to a strand of bacteria on a New Jersey beach the politics of Brazil."

"Yes, that would be absurd!" Tom said as they all laughed.

"Well, you see," Charles went on, "In the first place, strands of bacteria don't have the ability to receive such information, and even if they could, they would not have the means to understand the information they were given. So that you can better understand what I just told you," Charles continued, "I'll give you an illustration of how two different dimensions of space and time can co-exist. For instance Tom, see Mr. Pritchard out there fishing from his boat?"

Tom and Sharon watched as the solitary fisherman drifted slowly on the lake as he leisurely worked his fishing line.

"Suppose," Charles continued, "you took a picture of that boat and fisherman. The picture would consist of two dimensions, height and width. In reality the boat would be in our three-dimensional world of height, width, and depth. What if Mr. Pritchard had the ability to pass from the three dimensional boat into the two dimensional picture? That would be quite a feat, would it not?"

Charles watched the expressions on the two faces across the table from him. He could almost see the wheels of understanding turning. "Now suppose that someone could step from the real three-dimensional boat into dimensions beyond—or someone from dimensions beyond could step into the real boat."

"You're saying the horses and chariots of fire in Elisha's situation were from a dimension beyond the three we have now?"

"That's what I'm saying," Charles answered. "There are beings in other dimensions all around us, even as we speak. We just can't see them. Elisha's servant had to be allowed to see into another dimension."

"Are you saying that I saw into another dimension too?" asked Tom.

"Very likely," Charles replied. "There are dimensions beyond height, width, depth, and time, and on into the dimension of spirit where the Father and Creator live."

Sharon said, "You mean heaven?"

"Yes; I'm glad you understand that heaven is not so far away," Charles replied. "People have so many different concepts of heaven and where heaven is. Some think heaven is only way out where the stars are and only in a three-dimensional state. Things that are seen in the night sky-the stars, planets, galaxies-are still part of a three dimensional universe no matter how far away they are. God is of spirit. Heaven is of spirit. Heaven is closer than you think. Those who look for heaven only in these three dimensions will be sadly disappointed."

Tom said, "There is a project known as SETI, you know, the search for extra terrestrial intelligence. They've been using huge antennae arrays linked to super computers. Those computers search the heavens for any signs of electro magnetic communication among the stars. So far they haven't found anything."

Charles added, "Yes, and there is a project known as Operation Tablespoon being operated by your military to search the skies for anything moving in close proximity to the earth and billions of miles beyond. It is code named Tablespoon because it can record anything that approaches the earth larger in size than a tablespoon. This information is instantly transmitted to the computers at Operation Tablespoon headquarters located at Cheyenne Mountain in Colorado."

Tom said, "I've never heard of that."

"It's likely you've never heard of it. Your government doesn't like to talk about it. Neither do they like to talk about project Deep Blue, a series of super computers, which accumulate information on nearly every conceivable thing. These projects and others, in their search for intelligent life in the three dimensional universe, have discovered absolutely nothing. Industrialized nations all over the world have spent billions of dollars chasing their tails to learn no more than what they knew already. They are in the photograph trying to see into the real world. It can't be done. When this latest human effort to search for life in outer space, the Hubble telescope, sees as far as it can see, it will still find no one."

"If no one else is out there, then why is the universe so big?" Sharon pondered aloud.

"To illustrate the power and glory of the Creator of the universe!" exclaimed Charles. "You see, Sharon, communication beyond the three dimensional universe is not accomplished with super computers or the Hubble telescope. It is done with the heart and soul."

Dusk had again turned to darkness, penetrated only by the glow of dying charcoal and fireflies around the edge of the lake.

"So what are you saying?" Tom asked as he lit the camping lantern that hung on a post at the end of the picnic table.

"You see, Tom, misguided, but well-meaning people are using the Hubble telescope, gigantic radio receivers, and other means to find out if there is life out there. One thing that has been proven beyond any doubt by using these programs is that so-called aliens, UFOs and other unexplained phenomena did not come from outer space."

"So what are you really saying?" Tom asked.

"I am saying that your government is beginning to understand. They have now established ultra secret programs being funded to discover the source and means of travel from one dimension to another."

"How do you know all this," asked Sharon, "if it's ultra secret? And why are you telling us?"

"Our group does private investigations separate from any government involvement. And our information is not secret."

"You mean what happened to me in the meadow is travel from one dimension to another?"

"Yes," came Charles' reply. "That's exactly what I mean, Tom. Your government is going to great expense to investigate reports of incidents that match yours. They think they know the secret to these puzzling occurrences and are looking for the proof, but they can't seem to find it. You may be closer than you realize to something your government is investigating."

"Do you think my experience will be investigated?"

"Who knows?" Charles replied, but one thing is certain, your article in the paper has been reviewed and definitely alerted the government that the incident took place."

"Maybe if the government investigates, they might even tell me what really happened. Then I'd feel better about having a real answer."

"These points of transfer from one dimension to another can be numerous," Charles explained. "And you apparently live close to one of them. But don't count on your government to inform you of that."

Their attention was drawn momentarily to the fireflies as they made their otherwise invisible presence known for seconds at a time. The glow from the lantern lit the small area. A drifting breeze ushered in the cooler night air. While Sharon went inside the cabin to start a pot of coffee, Tom and Charles walked out onto the lawn to stretch their legs.

Looking up at the stars, Tom said, "You know, without the lights of the city to obscure them, stars are really bright, aren't they? They're amazing. I wonder...if there's no life as we know it out there, then what is?"

"No life as you can understand it," Charles answered. "However, there are many things out there in the spirit dimension."

"What about the Mars probe?" Tom asked. "They say they have found evidence, traces of micro life there."

"Well, that's what they say," replied Charles. "That rock on an ice field supposedly bounced here from Mars after a collision with an asteroid. Then there's that rock they found in the Sahara Desert. They claim it also came from Mars."

"You mean there is no evidence of life on Mars?"

"Let me put it to you this way, those managing the space program are of the evolutionary school of thought. From early childhood they were taught the evolutionary process. If non-factual evolutional information is taught consistently throughout their educational years, it will be believed."

"In other words, tell a lie big enough, long enough, and it will be believed," Tom questioned.

"Precisely! You see, Tom, these people have found yet another way to attempt to justify evolution. Some scientists now claim that life began on Mars and later came here. Who is going to prove them wrong? They hold the keys to the information! They hold the keys to the rockets!"

Charles continued, "Let me give you an example to prove the point. There is evidence all over the earth that a worldwide flood occurred a few thousand years ago. For example the evidence can be seen in the geological formations in the Grand Canyon. Evolutionists conclude that these formations took millions, if not billions, of years to form. Washington State's Mt. St. Helens exploded in 1980. In a matter of several hours, not millions of years, a one-fortieth scale model almost exactly duplicated the geological characteristics of the Grand Canyon. The replication is complete with varying strata and a gorge cut by massive amounts of floodwater. The Mt. St. Helen's event illustrated that the Grand Canyon could also have been similarly formed by a combination of violent volcanic activity and gigantic floodwaters in a very short period of time, not billions of years. Some scientists today assume that things changed in the past at the same speed that they change today. They are mistaken. The geological evidence is undeniable. When highway cuts in mountains expose sedimentary rock layers standing on their edges it is plain that violent crust movement has taken place in the past. Even though erosion is relatively slow now there have been past earth changes that took place suddenly and violently. See how thought manipulation can affect understanding of the truth?"

Tom said, "So I was right about telling a lie big enough, long enough and it will be believed. That's a pretty big lie!"

"That lie is what is being taught in most schools elementary through college," Charles related. "There is an unseen intelligence orchestrating the infiltration of this evolutionary idea into scientific thought. Satan, the Evil One, who is in opposition to the Creator, is coordinating the misinformation of evolution. The objective of this beguiler of men's souls is to turn the family of man from belief in the Creator by employing both subtle and blatant techniques. The evolutionary school of thought consists of both approaches. There is evidence in ancient written records from civilizations all over the earth to substantiate a worldwide flood. Evolutionists deny both the physical evidence and the ancient written records in their effort to promote their theory as fact. Scientists schooled in evolutionary thought used a miniature robot to explore a few square yards of the Martian surface. With a small amount of data, they determined in a matter of a few weeks that Mars has had an ancient planet-covering flood. Yet with a great quantity of physical and written evidence to support a worldwide flood on earth it is denied. With only a scant amount of information available, a Martian flood was heralded as a phenomenal discovery for science. In other words, governments all over the world are financing the religion of evolution."

"What do you mean the religion of evolution?" Sharon asked as she returned with a steaming pot of coffee and three cups. "You consider evolution a religion?"

"Evolution is indeed nothing more than a religion itself, or, actually, an anti-religion. Highly educated scientists corrupt pure analysis of data with evolutionary theory. Evolution is simply an unproven theory that postulates that the entire universe created itself and everything in it from the three dimensional perspective. Because of their naive thinking, it doesn't occur to them to investigate dimensions beyond the three that we can readily observe. A consequence of accepting evolutional theory, as fact, is that believers in evolution exempt themselves from a higher authority. The scientific community has convinced people that a Creator is not rationally required and does not exist. Evolution is theorized to have occurred over great expanses of time. The real creation requires a much shorter period of time. As recorded in ancient sacred writings, the Creator spoke and it came into being!"

"Wow! Look at that!" Tom pointed to a shooting star as it raced across the sky.

Charles and Sharon looked up in time to see a long trail across the night sky made by a meteor as it came to its fiery end, then another...and another...and yet another.

"The Creator is an awesome God," Charles said softly.

Tom replied, "Charles, you've talked about the Creator. Earlier tonight when you sang that beautiful song, you sang of the Redeemer. I thought God, the Father was the one who created. Are they all God?"

"The Father is the LORD of the entire universe and all its dimensions. He is referred to in English as God. By the authority of His Father, the Son created all things. You call Him the Word, the Messiah, the Christ. Most call Him Jesus."

"If you're saying that Jesus the Son is the Creator, then who are you saying is the Redeemer?"

"They're one and the same."

As the three watched the skies, a soft, white glow lit their faces. Suddenly the meteors increased in frequency until they reached a crescendo. Showers of brilliance lit the entire sky and cast radiance on the people sitting below.

Soon the meteor shower diminished and only the background of stars was visible. "You know," Charles said, "A day will come when stars will no longer be needed to declare the glory of God!"

One last meteor, much brighter than the others, seemed to end the display with a brilliant trail of light that extended from horizon to horizon.

Behind them the lantern popped and sputtered to announce that it was running low on fuel. None of the three had realized that the early morning hours had crept in.

"Charles?" Sharon reflected thoughtfully, "How do you know all this?"

"That's my job. That's what I do."

"Well, I don't think I have ever had such remarkable discussions," Tom remarked.

"It has been stimulating," Charles replied. "I have a long journey tomorrow so I must be on my way. Maybe we can meet here again."

"That would be wonderful!" Sharon expressed with a smile on her face.

"I'll be in touch," Charles told them.

"Goodnight, Charles," Tom called out as he stepped onto the porch. "And thanks for those big fish."

"My pleasure! Goodnight, you two."

Tom picked up the lantern and held onto the warm handle as he turned in Charles' direction. "Wait, Charles, you'll need to write down our address and phone...."

"Where did he go so quickly?" Tom wondered to himself. He set the lantern on the porch, made a mental note to fill it later when it had cooled off, and went into the cabin where Sharon had already started getting ready for bed.

As they settled in for a night's sleep, they commented to each other that Charles seemed to understand a lot about a myriad of things. "What did Charles mean about there being no need for stars anymore? I'll ask him about that when I give him our address tomorrow," Tom mumbled as he drifted off to sleep.

A sleepy "O.K." was Sharon's reply.

CHAPTER 10

The sunshine streamed in the open window, awakening the couple. Tom had promised Sharon a busy day of antique shopping on the way home so they didn't have time for sleeping in. However, late night discussions were not conducive to early rising. Reluctantly they got to their feet, yawning and stretching.

"Guess we need to get going," Tom spoke through his yawn as he headed toward the shower. "I'm going to Charles' cabin to give him our address," Tom announced above the sounds of the shower. "Do you want to come along?"

"Sure," Sharon replied, "After we get everything in order here."

Later when they walked to the edge of the front porch, Tom pointed toward the squirrel wheel and said, "Looks like we missed a good one; the corn is gone, the squirrels are gone, the show must be over."

"Seems like the squirrels always wait until we're not looking to go after the corn. I'd like to see that show just one time. Maybe next time we come we won't be so preoccupied."

"Yes, but a good preoccupation, wouldn't you agree?"

"Race you to the path!" Sharon yelled as she took off in a run.

Tom was quick but his late start still allowed Sharon to win. He took her by the hand and they jogged further down the path. They slowed to a walk as they got nearer to the place Sharon knew as the "rental" cabin. It got its name because it was the only cabin not lived in by its owners. Every summer, for as long as Sharon could remember, strangers came and went, much to the chagrin of the Pritchards who lived next door.

As the path took them closer, they could see that the rental cabin was in an appalling state of disrepair. Waist high weeds surrounded the place. Poison ivy wound about the milkweed. It appeared uninviting. As they got closer they saw that the steps were rickety and falling down. Weeds grew through cracks in the floorboards on the wobbly, unsteady front porch. The screen door hinge at the top was rusted and broken. The door sagged to one side. Tom brushed spider webs aside. As he knocked on the door broken glass in the window rattled and a musty odor rushed out of the cabin.

A voice from behind them said, "No one's there."

Tom and Sharon turned from the front door to see Mr. and Mrs. Pritchard standing in the yard at the edge of the porch.

"We're looking for a man named Charles who's been staying here the last few days."

A puzzled look came over the faces of the two older people.

The woman answered, "Why honey, no one's stayed in this cabin for over five years."

CHAPTER 11

⊬⊨⊣

As Tom and Sharon approached downtown and saw the familiar skyline of Indianapolis, they knew home was just a few miles away. It had been a pleasant trip traveling back from their stay at the lake. As planned, they made several stops at antique shops along the way.

Tom started with, "No matter how good a time you have on vacation…"

"It's always good to come home," Sharon finished.

They still wondered about their mysterious friend Charles Levi. Where did he come from? Where did he stay? Where did he go? He had been the topic of conversation all the way home.

After a long pause, Sharon flipped on the radio.

…*"on sale only this week you can have…clearing skies and cooling temperatures tonight…in sports today…questioned the Chinese about their intentions. But the reliable Abrams Report discloses that in addition to all the other things that the Chinese have planned, they also plan to invade and take over Taiwan. According to the Abrams Report their information sources are absolutely reliable. You people had better…Indy's oldies, five in a row on the Gold 45 station…"*

"Now, that's better!" Sharon said, satisfied with her favorite station.

They turned off I-70 onto Highway 93 and soon passed the Brown's farmhouse. Arlin and Maggie were walking from the barn toward the house. Tom tooted the horn and waved as they drove by.

No sooner had the T-bird turned into the driveway than Tom and Sharon saw the Nicholsons on their way across the road to meet them. They seemed to be in a hurry. Tom waved and indicated that he would meet them at the garage. Tom stopped the car in front of the garage door. Sharon reached for the door opener and the cell phone fell out of the compartment. She had forgotten it was there. Tom opened the trunk as Sharon opened the garage door.

"We're glad you're back," Linda said as they greeted each other warmly.

"Glad to be home. How would you like some fresh bass?" Tom asked as he lifted the cooler lid. "I've got some right here."

Sharon dug through the ice to find one of the packages of fish and held the large plastic bag out to Andy.

"Dad, look at this! Where did you get such big fish?"

"It's a long story. We'll have a fish fry and tell you all about it. There are a couple of pictures I'd like you to see...one in particular."

"It's a deal," Linda said as she sent her son home with their share of fish to put in the freezer. "Oh, Andy, bring their mail back too."

"Hey, Tom, that redness in your face has faded. Most people get a tan on vacation. You lose yours," Andy called out on his way home with the fish.

"By the way, we have a story to tell you guys!" Steve said.

"Come on in the house where it's cool and tell us all about it."

Tom drove the car into the garage, took the suitcase from the trunk, maneuvered his way through the mudroom and started down the hall. He suddenly stopped short.

"What is this?" he said as he set the suitcase on the floor.

He and Sharon examined broken pieces of plastic on the carpet. They looked up near the ceiling to see that the smoke detector had been smashed. Sharon picked up a brass candlestick lying nearby. "This must have been used as a hammer."

"Steve!" Tom shouted. "Look at this!"

Steve and Linda hurried down the hall.

"What happened?" they questioned in unison.

As they walked down the hall, Sharon noticed the condition of the bedroom. She muffled a cry as her hand flew to her mouth.

"Why didn't the alarm go off?" Tom murmured as anger built inside. "We'd better call the sheriff."

They began checking the other rooms of the house. They were all trashed. It was Linda who stepped into the living room. Everyone heard her gasp.

"Come here!" she shouted. "You won't believe this!"

The other three rushed to the living room to see a gaping hole in the floor and furniture in disarray.

"What is going on? What do we have that anybody would want?" Sharon asked. "And why did they cut a hole in our living room floor?"

"...That's how they got in. So they wouldn't trip the alarm." Tom exclaimed as his anger continued to build. "Come on, Steve, I think I know how they did this."

He and Steve hurried outside to the back of the house as Sharon hurried to the phone to call the sheriff.

At the crawl space door Tom's suspicions were confirmed. The door stood open.

"The only place in the house not wired to the alarm. I thought we had it all covered!" Tom lamented to Steve.

Sharon and Linda joined the men. "I called the sheriff's office. Somebody should be here in a few minutes."

Steve took a deep breath and hesitated, "I think I know who did this."

"...Oh! The black Mercedes!" Linda interjected.

"Yeah, the black Mercedes," Steve regretfully admitted as he told the story of the encounter with the man who claimed to be a CIA agent. Andy joined them and agreed with his father's story by constantly nodding his head as Steve talked. When Steve finished, Andy told how he had patiently kept the red dot on the trespasser's shirt but kept his finger off the trigger just as his dad had taught him.

They all walked back into the house to wait for the sheriff. After looking at the floor again Steve and Tom agreed it must have been the work of a chain saw. The two- cycle engine must have pumped the house full of smoke. That would account for the smashed smoke detector. Sharon burst into tears at the sight of saw teeth marks on her antique school desk. Tom put his arm around her and said, "Sorry honey," as he tried to console her. "Let the cops see it just like it is so they can look for evidence."

"Who would do this to our house and why?" Sharon asked again.

In ten minutes a deputy sheriff's car pulled into the driveway. The deputy came in, looked at the damage and then asked, "What are you missing?"

"Well, we haven't discovered anything missing."

After listening to Steve's story, the sheriff's deputy went back out to his car to call for Sheriff Carter.

"He'll be here in about half an hour," the deputy said when he returned.

When Sheriff Carter arrived, he remarked to Tom, "Investigations are becoming a habit in this neighborhood."

"Not by choice, I assure you!" Tom replied.

The next three hours under Sheriff Carter's supervision, his men dusted for fingerprints, took pictures and gathered evidence. During the investigation, once again, Steve related his story about the suspicious behavior of the man who identified himself as J.T. Williamson, a CIA agent. Investigators discovered Sharon's jewelry scattered over the bedroom floor. Clothes had been dumped out of the drawers and drawers appeared to be tossed at random on the floor. In the process a deputy discovered, in plain sight, $200 in "mad money" Sharon kept in a dresser.

"If it wasn't money or jewelry they were after, then what?" the deputy asked as he scratched behind his ear. "This is a real puzzler."

"You know, it makes you wonder," the sheriff said as an afterthought. "This break-in seems as strange as the break-in at the county coroner's office. That body bag we put in the cooler is gone. Wonder if the guy in the black Mercedes had anything to do with that?"

"Oh yes!" Sharon recalled. "As we left for our trip to the lake, we passed a black Mercedes parked at the gate to the meadow."

Sheriff Carter began trying to put pieces of the puzzle together. "It looks as if we need to find our guy in the black Mercedes. I'll get right on it. I think we've done all we can here for now. You folks do what you want to fix this mess. I hope we can catch whoever did this to your place."

"We do too," Sharon said in a voice that was no longer so much hurt or scared, but angry.

After the sheriff left, Steve, Andy, and Tom secured the crawl space door. Tom called a carpenter he knew to do repairs on the floor. He assured Tom he would be over the next morning. Sharon made arrangements to have new carpet delivered, and then announced that she was angry and really didn't know what to do about it.

Tom responded, "I'm just as mad as you! I know what to do about it, too. The problem is the guy who did this isn't around for me to hit!"

"Tom, I feel really bad about the break-in. I was supposed to be watching the house for you," Steve said.

"Steve, don't worry about it, I know you can't stare at the house day and night. Obviously whoever broke in here did it by sneaking in so no one would see them."

"You're probably right," Steve said. "But that doesn't make me feel much better. Anyway I think I've let you guys down. How about if you two spend the night at our house?"

"Thanks, but we'd better stay here. Besides, if they come back while we're at your house, there would be nobody here to shoot them."

"Tom, you wouldn't shoot anybody," Sharon said.

"Watch me! If there's someone in the house doing..."

"Well, maybe," Sharon relented.

Tom nodded at Steve knowingly. He and Steve had fired weapons in battle before. They both knew the drill. Steve knew very well that under proper conditions, Tom would pull the trigger, without hesitation.

When the Nicholsons left, Tom went straight for his hidden 9mm pistol and put it under his pillow...loaded. Sharon didn't have to know.

After some of their restlessness wore off, Tom and Sharon went to bed. Sharon slipped her hand under Tom's pillow and felt the cold metal pistol. "I knew you would do that. After all, you are my knight in shining armor."

CHAPTER 12

Sharon and Tom moved furniture out of the living room and into other parts of the house. They could feel a springing action in the floor, weakened by the cut floor joists, as they walked around the hole in the living room.

Each time she passed the hole in the floor, Sharon's anger escalated. The floor could be repaired and so could the carpet. But Sharon couldn't shake the feeling of being violated by strangers. She looked at the splintered wood in the saw marks on her antique school desk. With an ache in her heart, she remembered the countless hours she and Tom had spent in various antique shops to find this vintage desk.

Tom didn't have very much to say aloud. Thoughts raced through his mind. He was trying to understand what someone could possibly want from his house. Aside from the general mess of the room, his computer CD cabinets were open and his CDs were strewn around the room.

When all the furniture was removed from the living room, Tom and Sharon gathered the CDs and arranged them back in order. They found themselves looking around the now- empty room and trying to make sense of it all when the doorbell rang. Preoccupied, they had missed the sound of Cecil Rhodes' truck as he drove into the driveway. The carpenter arrived just as he said he would at 8:00 with lumber to repair the living room floor.

Cecil and his assistant pulled the damaged carpet loose from the floor, rolled it up and lugged it out the front door into the yard. The old carpet would be disposed of later. Steve and Andy saw the activity from their front porch and offered to help.

While Cecil and his helper installed new carpet, Tom and Steve with Andy's help, secured the crawl space door and ran a wire from the alarm to a switch on the door. Someone may open the door again but at least the alarm will sound, Tom reasoned.

Unnoticed and well hidden in the tall grass on the gentle, sloping hill behind the house, two mysterious figures observed the activities below with much curiosity. Their acute hearing was sensitive to the slightest sound. Their keen eyesight recorded movements they didn't understand. They patiently waited.

"The repairs were really no big deal," Cecil said as he charged Tom a surprisingly small fee for the work. Cecil said his goodbyes then packed up his gear and left for another job.

As the door closed, the phone rang. Tom answered. It was the office manager from the Hoosier Tribune calling to see if Tom had returned from vacation. She told him that Sam was in the hospital. Tom was startled to learn that his office had been ransacked just as his house had been and that the break-in was the cause of Sam's hospitalization. They talked for a while, discussing similarities of the two break-ins. He learned that rumors abounded downtown.

"Sharon, you know Sam, the custodian at the Tribune? He's in the hospital. And get this; there was a break in at my office while we were gone. The place was ransacked just like it was here." Tom wondered why the sheriff hadn't mentioned the break-in at his office. Then it occurred to him the investigation at the office would be handled by the city police and not the county sheriff. Besides, they weren't even in the same county. To the two different law enforcement agencies, each was a separate crime. But Tom recognized that both assaults were on him. There had to be a connection. Tom decided to call the sheriff and tell him that he suspected both crimes might have been committed by the same person. "Evidently somebody thinks I have something worth stealing, but what could it possibly be?"

"Sharon, I want to go check on Sam," Tom suggested to Sharon.

Still at their vantage point on the slope, the two inquisitive figures peered through the tall grass as the T-bird pulled out of the driveway. The stranded beings had no choice but to continue to wait for an opportunity to escape back into their domain.

In a downtown Indianapolis hotel suite, government agents had been poring over videotapes taken from the Apache reconnaissance helicopters. A team of investigators led by J.T. Williamson had been working hard for two days repeatedly viewing the tapes. A phone call to J.T. from his boss George in Fairfax provided critical information for the team that immediately and completely changed the direction of the hunt. Finally they found their clue. Very, very faintly in the thermal imaging videos the patterns of two figures were seen hiding in the trees. It was not understood how the figures were able to nearly defeat the thermal imaging detectors. What was important though was that videos from two of the helicopters verified each other and the images could be seen. Somehow these figures had assumed very nearly the same temperature as the trees and the slight temperature difference could scarcely be detected from the monitors inside the helicopters. But after hours of close scrutiny the videotapes released their secret. The surveillance by the Apaches was not a waste and the stage was set.

As Tom and Sharon entered the downtown area the top-of-the hour newscast was relating stories of unrest in most major cities in the United States. American Jews and sympathizers to the Jewish situation were conducting open demonstrations in the streets, proclaiming their support for Israel's right to build a temple in Jerusalem. Also they were demanding that the United States honor its commitment to defend Israel in case of attack. Leadership in the United States was more willing to listen to their pleas in view of the events of that fateful day in September 2001. Rhetoric from nations that supported Islamic terrorism was intensifying. Friends of Israel around the world were becoming more outspoken in their concern. It seemed that peaceful people were looking to the United States to diffuse the conflict. Before the newscaster completed the broadcast, Sharon reached over and turned the radio off. Tom understood that such things upset Sharon. They finished the drive to the hospital in silence.

When they arrived at Sam's hospital room, he was sitting up in bed with a big smile on his face, looking the picture of health. Sam greeted them as they came into the room. "I want you to meet my son, Willie," Sam said as he motioned to a tall, muscular, handsome black man who rose from a chair facing Sam's bed. The silver eagles on the collar of his uniform indicated that he was a full Colonel.

"I thought you said your son was a Lieutenant Colonel?" remarked Tom as he extended his hand in greeting.

The uniformed man spoke in a deep voice, "Only last week the promotion came through. New job. New rank." As they shook hands, he continued, "Will Keller. You must be Tom Alexander."

"So you're the Colonel William Keller that I've heard so much about. This is my wife, Sharon."

"How do you do, ma'am?"

"Fine thanks, but please call me Sharon."

"Tom, I feel as if I've known you for years. My dad has been talking about you ever since I arrived. We've been trying to determine why your desk was the focus of the break-in at the office."

"We've been trying to understand the same thing."

"My dad tells me they were looking for your medallion."

"My medallion? What medallion? "

"The man who broke in said he wanted your medallion, Mr. Tom."

"I don't know anything about a medallion."

"Oh, so that's why my jewelry box was dumped out. He must have been looking for the medallion at our house too," Sharon said.

"He broke into your house?" Sam exclaimed.

"Somebody did and he ripped up the place pretty good, too."

Tom and Sharon filled them in on some of the particulars, including their neighbors' story of the confrontation on Tom's property with the man who said he was a CIA agent. At the mention of the CIA, Will's expression changed and he was intent on Tom's every word. He did not comment, however. As the discussion continued Tom observed that Will was interested in every detail. After a long conversation about the break-in, Tom recalled why he and Sharon had come to the hospital in the first place.

"How are you doing, Sam?" Tom asked, apologizing for not asking sooner. "You seem so healthy and happy that I didn't think to ask about you were feeling."

"No need to apologize, Mr. Tom. I am happy. The doctors tell me that my heart is doing fine and all I need is a couple of days rest. The main reason that I feel good is because Willie is here. I haven't seen him since last fall. Being with my kid is like medicine to me."

Will smiled at his dad. He was relieved that his dad was doing well and it was good to be home. While he was sorry for the reason that brought him here, he welcomed the diversion from the pressures of his Washington duties.

Tom observed that Will seemed to be a kind and gentle man who obviously loved his dad very much. As Tom stood up to leave, he reached out his hand to shake Will's. "You guys have some catching up to do. We'll be on our way."

Before Will could respond, Tom added, "Oh, by the way, do you know anything about something called Operation Tablespoon?"

Will's grip tightened on Tom's hand. He had been actively involved in the classified Operation Tablespoon for the last 15 years. His smile faded to a surprised frown and he replied, "How do you know about Operation Tablespoon?"

Tom was taken aback by the sudden change in Will's demeanor. Their hands parted as Tom started to explain.

"We'd better sit down for this," Tom said as he sat back down in his chair.

Sharon and Will followed suit. Tom began by telling of the chance meeting with Charles and repeated what he was told about Operation Tablespoon and Project Deep Blue. Will's eyes narrowed as he wondered how Charles knew so much about highly classified information. He had not been briefed on any think tank that had access to that information. It wasn't top secret but it wasn't for general public consumption either. Will was aware that it was common knowledge the government had spent considerable time and resources investigating reports of extraterrestrial travel. What the public did not know was that Operation Tablespoon compiled hard data that proved beyond any doubt that extraterrestrial visits were real, but that the visitors do not come from space. Investigations into UFOs found the U.S. government investigating itself. The UFO phenomenon began as a disinformation tool used by the military to deflect public interest away from the development of ultra secret aircraft testing. It had grown from an intentional diversion into a public obsession. It was successful beyond the wildest dreams of those who conceived it. Operations such as Tablespoon were being shut down as the focus was being redirected at dimensional shifts rather than space travel. Will had been encouraged to join the new search, instead of retiring. The FBI and CIA were being called in to investigate suspicious reports. Will perceived that if he prompted him, Tom could possibly feed him some valuable information. But because the prompts would be of classified nature, Will chose to remain silent.

Tom also chose to remain silent about his encounter at the meadow and the bizarre occurrences there. He had no idea that Will was assigned to investigate the very thing that Tom had experienced. They were a handshake away from full discovery — a discovery that could have led to the debunking of many myths and legends.

During the discussion, Will asked several unanswerable questions about Charles. Even though they told him all they knew, Charles was still a man of mystery.

As they left, Tom and Sharon wished Sam a speedy recovery. Sam's smile added a few more lines to his wrinkled face.

The couple walked into the daylight in silence and made their way to the car. The T-bird gracefully wound through outbound traffic on I-70 West toward home. The sun rested low in the afternoon sky. Tom pulled the sun visor down to protect his eyes. He moved to the middle lane of the three-lane highway and was passing a long line of trucks that were in the right lane. Sharon glanced in Tom's direction and gasped as she grabbed his arm. Tom looked quickly to his left to see what had caught her attention. There in the next lane, matching their speed was the infamous black Mercedes. A heavily tinted window on the passenger's door moved down and the driver pointed a gun in their direction. The driver planned to intimidate Tom into pulling over. The plan didn't work. Tom looked for an escape. From his low-slung car he could see under the semi trailers to his right. There was an exit ramp ahead. Thoughts of the past few days rushed through his mind. The black Mercedes was trouble.

Tom didn't have to think long. His foot went to the floor. The

T-bird lunged forward. Tom pulled hard to the right on the steering wheel. The car dove between two semis with only inches to spare, then onto the exit ramp. Tom's sudden maneuver caught the Mercedes driver by surprise. There was not enough time or space for the Mercedes to perform the same maneuver. It had to pass the exit. Once on the ramp Tom pushed hard on the brakes. He slowed and made the right turn onto Afton Street below. His heart sank as he saw road construction and a traffic jam ahead. The escape was blocked. There was nowhere for a candy apple red '57 Thunderbird to hide among the many stopped late model vehicles. Thinking quickly, Tom reasoned that whoever was in the Mercedes would go to the next interchange, turn around, and drive back, then find them trapped in traffic. Tom decided to make a quick U-turn on Afton Street, get back on the interstate and meet the Mercedes coming from the opposite direction. He hoped this would buy more time. As he entered I-70 West, he once again floored the gas pedal. Sharon gripped the armrest tightly. Tension in her body stiffened her back. Once on the interstate, Tom looked to his left to see the Mercedes approaching on the eastbound side. Tom had miscalculated. A cloud of dust hanging between the lanes ahead confirmed that the Mercedes had made a U-turn on the median instead of going to the next interchange. Tom realized that the time interval between the two vehicles would be much shorter than he had anticipated.

The Mercedes decelerated down the exit ramp and made a left turn on Afton Street, encountering the same traffic jam that had impeded the T-bird. With the two left wheels up on the curb, the Mercedes threaded its way between traffic and barricades. It passed the line of stopped cars that were underneath the overpass, sideswiping one car in the process. It made a left turn and roared onto the entrance ramp to I-70 West and was once again in pursuit of the T-bird.

Tom maneuvered expertly through traffic on the interstate. Glancing in the rear view mirror, he switched to the left lane where he could travel faster. Over the roar of the engine and the wind, the two debated their situation. They wondered who the guy was in the black Mercedes, why he was chasing them with a gun, what the medallion was, and why he wanted it. "Why does this guy think we have it?" They realized that whatever he wanted, he was serious about it, or he would not have pulled a gun on them. With no weapon in the car for their defense, the only option they had was to try to escape.

The T-bird quickly increased speed to 120, then 140 where the speedometer pegged. The car continued to accelerate. Now, Tom was becoming concerned about the car as it sped beyond 140 mph. Faster and faster, the speed climbed. Tom held his foot to the floor. The car still continued to accelerate. He knew the car would go faster still, but he questioned whether it was able to hold the road at an even higher speed. Aerodynamic principles flashed through his mind. If enough air got under the car it could take off like an aircraft without wings and come to a deadly end. Tom knew what the suspension felt like when the car's wheels left the pavement. He was getting dangerously close to that point.

Suddenly a violent vibration shook the car. Tom let off the gas and gripped the steering wheel tightly. Sharon groped for something to hold on to. For the next mile or so they were in fear for their lives. If they continued to accelerate, the car could crash. If they slowed down they would risk being shot. As suddenly as it started, the vibration stopped. The car had slowed to 110. Tom glanced in his rear view mirror. The black dot he saw off in the distance told him that the Mercedes was hot after them. With less than a quarter of a tank of gas left, he knew the chase could end in a predictable manner. He gripped the steering wheel tighter and formed a plan in his mind. Over the road noise Tom shouted to Sharon to get out the cell phone.

"Call Jim and tell him we need to use his garage — quick."

Sharon nervously pulled out the phone and realized that she didn't know his number. Tom couldn't remember it either. "What a time to go brain dead!" Tom thought. He knew Jim Newland's number as well as he knew his own. Sharon came to the rescue. She simply called information to ask for the number.

"Good thinking!" Tom shouted over the roar in the car. "You may have just saved our lives!"

The wind in the speeding car blew hard against the cell phone in her hand. Highway 93 was coming up fast. Sharon managed to punch in the number. After four rings, Jim answered.

"Jim!" Sharon shouted into the phone. "This is Sharon."

"Sharon, what's wrong?"

"Please don't ask any questions. This is an emergency. Listen to me. We need to hide our car in your garage quick. Can you help us?"

"Sure, you can park your car here anytime. What's going on?"

"Listen to me Jim; this could be life or death. I don't have time to explain. We're being chased by some idiot down I-70 and we're almost to 93. Please make a place for us in your garage!"

Sensing the urgency of the situation Jim told Sharon that the door would be open by the time they got there. He hung up the phone and immediately went to work making a space.

Tom unclenched his jaw a bit. He almost breathed a sigh of relief. Sharon turned to look down the highway behind them. She saw that the Mercedes was hot after them and gaining. Tom noticed it too. The Mercedes must be doing at least 130, Tom estimated. He was afraid to go any faster because of the way the car buffeted as it sliced through turbulent air. He didn't want to lose control.

Tom entered the exit ramp at an excessive rate of speed. He stood on the brakes. If he could make the turn onto 93 without being seen, the Mercedes driver wouldn't know whether they went left or right. Instead of making a right turn to go to their house, Tom made a left turn in the direction of Jim's garage. He pressed the accelerator to the floor and pulled down on the speed shift. The rear tires were spinning as if they were on ice. The speedometer once again pegged at 140. Tom shifted gears. The car's forward speed was about 15 miles per hour. Carburetors and engine roared. Hot tires screamed on the pavement. Blue gray oily smoke boiled from the rear wheel wells. The whole rear end of the car disappeared into the blue cloud. Tom realized his mistake and released pressure from the accelerator. As the wheels slowed their spin, the tires grabbed asphalt. The car surged forward as if it had been slung from a catapult. Tom pressed the accelerator again. The roar of the engine and the scream of burning tires made a deafening sound as the car sped under the I-70 overpass. The concrete reverberated from the sound of the powerful engine. Tom had never given his T-bird such punishment. Like a rocket, the car sped to the next intersection on the right, where he turned onto the road to Jim's. Tom slowed abruptly once again to make the sharp right turn.

The Mercedes had entered the exit ramp at a high rate of speed and came to a sliding stop at the end of the ramp. It wasn't difficult for the Mercedes driver to decide which way to turn. Tom and Sharon may as well have set up a neon sign that said, "They went that-a-way!" with a flashing arrow that pointed left. A surly grin came over J.T. Williamson's face as he looked at the blue cloud of rubber smelling smoke that hung in the air and the two black streaks scorched out on the pavement to the left. "How sly," J.T. muttered, "they're not going home." He caught a glimpse of red as the T- bird disappeared around the corner a half-mile ahead. They had almost gotten away.

When Tom made the right turn his foot again pushed the pedal to the floor. He raced another quarter mile to the entrance to Jim's garage just as Jim rolled a car out to make room. Tom rushed the T-bird into the garage as Jim brought the door down.

Once the car was inside the garage all three people rushed to the window in Jim's office and looked out. They could see the black Mercedes approaching Jim's at a high rate of speed with an Indiana State Police vehicle in hot pursuit. As the Mercedes flashed by Jim's driveway the driver could be seen pounding the steering wheel with his fist.

"Whew!" Tom said as he sagged into a chair beside Jim's desk. Sharon was pale and weak as she slid down the wall to sit on the floor.

"I need to call the sheriff, Jim."

Tom spent several minutes on the phone with Sheriff Carter. He reported all the details of the encounter with the Mercedes as the others listened intently.

As Tom and Sheriff Carter were about to wrap up their conversation, the sheriff said. "Hang on a minute. Tom, you'll be interested in this. We just received a radio report from the State Police that said the police cruiser that was chasing the Mercedes ran off the road and the Mercedes got away."

"Oh, man, now what?" Tom thought as he hung up the phone. He related the sheriff's story to the others.

Jim sniffed the air, "Smell that hot rubber?"

"It's my tires. There may not be any tread left on them."

Jim stepped to the door of his office and looked out into the garage at the T-bird. He called back over his shoulder, "You've really done it now buddy! Look what you've done to our car!"

Tom bolted to the door, followed by Sharon. The garage was filled with a blue haze from the still-smoking tires. The odor of burnt rubber was pungent. They heard the last whisper of air hiss from the flattened left rear tire. As the haze began to clear they could see that the wheel cover and fender skirt were both missing.

"Oh, no," Sharon said. "That's what that vibration was."

As Tom caressed the dents in the left rear fender, he remarked that at high speed the wheel cover must have come off, cutting the tire and knocking the fender skirt loose. Tom reasoned that when the wind caught the skirt it was slammed back into the fender, which would account for the dents.

"Somewhere out on I-70 is my wheel cover and fender skirt," Tom said as he bemoaned the condition of his car. "This black stuff all over the back of the car has to be burned tires."

"What is going on with you two? It seems that the last week you have had more adventure than most people have in a lifetime," Jim wisecracked.

"You don't know the half of it," Tom countered.

"There's more?" Jim asked.

Tom and Sharon told the story of the chance meeting at the lake with the mysterious Charles. They also related the news of the break-ins at their home and Tom's office. "And, to top it all," Tom declared, "A friend is in the hospital because of the same moron that chased us down the highway. For some reason he thinks I have some kind of medallion."

"Gee, buddy, you need to get a life! The one you've got is such a bore!"

Jim offered to take them home and assured them that within a week he could have the T-bird back in showroom condition.

As they left the garage, Jim commented to Tom, "Buddy, you put a bunch of bugs out of their misery on that windshield."

"Í wish that was all the damage there was!" Tom replied.

As they walked toward Jim's car, Tom nervously looked up and down the road. No sign of the Mercedes or the police.

"What a day!"

"What next?" Tom wondered. "And why us?"

CHAPTER 13

T om had reason to feel safe and secure. He had made certain
that the alarm covered every possible entrance into the house.
He had loaded weapons at the ready. Steve and Andy were on alert.
Still, Tom slept restlessly.

He awoke just at daybreak. He lay in bed silently and listened as
chirping birds re-established their territories for the day. The resi-
dent mockingbird began his customary morning ritual, first singing
from the rooftop, then from the maple tree and repeating his song
on the fence at the edge of the garden. As Sharon slept Tom quietly
got dressed and went to the kitchen. He turned on the radio and
lowered the volume so Sharon would not be awakened. Military
officials from the Pentagon were announcing their great concern
that the Iranian submarine, dubbed the 504, had not been located.
Tom wondered why this would cause the military such distress. He
then remembered from an earlier broadcast that the Iranians had
sworn to destroy Israel and had announced that the submarine was
their weapon of choice. The Pentagon officials reported that an
extensive search for the nuclear missile carrying 504 was underway
and was led by the U.S. Navy P-3 Orion antisubmarine aircraft.
Tom contemplated his days in the Second Gulf War and in the War
on Terrorism and wondered how this activity in the Mideast would
affect American lives. He understood that if the Iranian threats were
carried out, world peace was at great risk. He also knew that by
using the P-3 Orions in the hunt, the Navy was using its best. He

felt comforted by that.

As Tom poured water into a glassful of ice, he looked out the window. He could visualize the scene earlier when Andy had hidden in the vegetable garden with his gun sights on the intruder. The morning mist still hung close to the ground in the low places near the garden.

Tom finished his last sip of water, and then walked into the garden. The birds suddenly stopped singing. The abrupt silence grabbed Tom's attention. They sensed danger. Tom felt rather than heard a very low frequency vibration. It wasn't a loud sound, but it was enough to get his attention. He had heard that sound before. Tom's train of thought was broken when Sharon called out to him from the kitchen window that Arlin Brown was on the phone.

Arlin remembered Steve's account of the CIA man and the Mercedes. His voice was excited as he told Tom that the Mercedes was back at the meadow and the driver was standing by the car looking through binoculars in the direction of the woods. Arlin had already called the sheriff. And he told Tom that the deputies were on the way.

Tom hung up the phone and started to tell Sharon what was happening. Immediately the phone rang again. This time it was Steve. "Tom!" Steve shouted into the phone. "There's an Apache Longbow hovering behind my trees. It's looking in the direction of the meadow."

Now it was confirmed; the low frequency sound Tom had heard while he was in the garden was the beat of a hovering helicopter rotor.

"Wait a minute!" Steve said after a second look, "I thought it was a Longbow but it's not. This Apache is different somehow. I don't really know what it is. It's different. And it's just hovering. They're looking for something in the meadow. Wonder what the big attraction is?"

Steve was correct. This helicopter was not an Apache Longbow. It was the army's newest helicopter, a Keowah. Inside, the crew was watching their sophisticated scanner consoles and looking for specific hard-to-find images. They had reviewed previously recorded videotapes from the Longbow. Two creatures in the woods could be seen on the monitors if you knew what to look for. They had brought in a helicopter with top-secret equipment aboard to do what the Longbow couldn't do – find the creatures in the woods.

"Are you calling on a cell phone?" Tom asked. "If you are, they can track you."

"Can't track this baby," Steve replied. "It's a random digital remote. Besides they're not scanning the area. They're looking at a specific spot. They must be hunting for something important or they wouldn't have brought in this expensive equipment to find it."

"Stay put!" Tom told Sharon as he rushed out of the house.

"You're not leaving me here by myself! I'm going with you!"

Tom saw the determined look on her face, "All right. I'll tell you what's happening on the way."

Unknown to Arlin, Steve, or Tom, there were two hovering Blackhawk helicopters two miles away, each with ten men on board awaiting a command from the Apache to descend to the landing zone.

As Tom and Sharon left their driveway in the Ranger, they could see Steve and Andy running from the woods at the edge of the cornfield toward Steve's house. Tom turned down the road in the direction of the meadow. He knew that Steve would be close behind.

Tom and Sharon approached the meadow and from a distance they recognized the menacing black Mercedes that had chased them into Jim's garage. It was parked on the edge of the road near the entrance to the meadow. As they came nearer they observed the serenity of the meadow and the surrounding area, a sharp contrast to the unexplained chaos that Tom had encountered a few nights before. The cut-off fence posts lying near the gate and the groove cut in the bank above the ditch were reminders that the incident was not a dream.

The sheriff's car drove through the gate and slid to a stop. A man in a dark suit walking near the middle of the grassy meadow scarcely noticed. His attention was directed toward the woods. As Tom and Sharon cautiously stepped out of the truck, they wondered if the man was the same one who had pointed the gun at them.

Their thoughts were interrupted by the deep resonating pulse of two Blackhawk helicopters, approaching at low level from behind the wooded area. The Blackhawks rushed to their landing zones on opposite sides of the woods and hovered just above the ground. As the wash from the rotors blew the tall grass in rippling waves, armed soldiers began jumping out before the helicopters touched the ground. Directed by the crew in the Apache, the two groups of soldiers approached their target in the center of the woods.

Sharon pointed to the top of the hill. Arlin was in his front yard taping the whole scene with a video recorder. The tranquility of the meadow had once again been shattered by turmoil.

Steve, Andy and Linda drove through the gate, into the meadow and parked beside Tom and Sharon's truck. A Keowah helicopter roared in low overhead from behind. It took up a hovering position to scan the woods. The reverberation from rotors pounding the air was intense. Both Tom and Steve understood that this maneuver was not just a Keowah crew gathering data. This was an infantry platoon operation. Steve shouted to Tom above the roar, "These guys mean business!" What kind of business neither man knew.

All the spectators in the disquieting scene watched as two odd gray creatures emerged from their hiding places in the woods. The creatures ran straight toward the man in the middle of the meadow. With the flushing of the creatures, the soldiers assumed success. Actually, the soldiers' presence was merely incidental. The gray creatures had their own agenda and were exerting every effort to make a rendezvous.

Tom shouted to Steve, "Is that our man?"

Suddenly, Steve recognized the dark-suited man as J.T. Williamson. Steve turned, cupped his hands around his mouth and called out to the sheriff's deputies over the sound of the helicopters, "That's him! That's him! That's the man! His name is J.T. He's the one who broke into Tom's house! Arrest him!"

At Steve's insistence, the deputies ran in J.T.'s direction. J.T. however was otherwise occupied. He called upon his experience as a college football player, intercepted and tackled the strange gray creature that held the elusive gold medallion. Once the creature was down, J.T. removed the gold medallion from his victim's hand. His attention had been so focused on his prey that he had not noticed two sheriff's deputies bearing down on him, one with a drawn pistol, the other with cuffs in hand. He held the medallion at arm's length, jumped a foot off the ground and shouted, "I've got it!" CRACK!!!

A dazzling flash of light and a thunderous noise pierced the meadow. Startled, Tom and Sharon ducked their heads as they quickly turned in the direction of the noise. Tom grew tense as he looked at the scene ahead. With no hesitation, he put his arm around Sharon and threw them both face-down on the ground. The screen was back. The two creatures dashed quickly across the meadow and disappeared into the screen. Even in daylight Tom could see movement in the brightly lit screen area he saw that fateful night. Suddenly, warriors, their features indistinguishable because of the smoky haze and bright light, waged a battle within the depths of the screen. Rumbling sounds shook the ground.

Once again Tom heard the same strange and eerie sound, as if rusty nails were being pulled from hardwood. A stray beam of light emanated from the screen, striking the ground in the meadow. Grass, dirt and sod flew upward as the beam plowed and gouged, leaving smoke and a burnt stench to drift in the air. Deep within the screen, other beams of light seemed to blaze at random as the battle raged on.

Tom pulled Sharon closer in a protective embrace and shouted above the intermittent booming noise. "Those beams are like the one I saw that night!"

Sharon was too numbed by the encounter to respond. She clung tightly to Tom for security and protection.

They shielded their eyes as brilliance radiated from the screen. With apprehension they watched as a mysterious flying craft rushed out of the screen and proceeded directly toward them. Never quite touching the ground, it stopped a few yards away. The craft's form was roughly the shape of a ski boat. It was about 20 feet long, shaped to a point on the bow and square across the stern. Other craft followed and gave chase in the skies around the area. Tom and Sharon's attention was drawn to the impressive craft that floated directly in front of them. The craft was mother of pearl in color with a clear dome that extended from bow to stern. The pilot was wearing clothes that appeared translucent, but the glow came from within and was ethereal in nature. Tom looked at the pilot who seemed strangely familiar. Tom heard Sharon shout the name "Charles?" Then again, "Charles!" a little louder. Charles smiled, evidently pleased that he was so easily recognized by Sharon. He motioned for them to come nearer as his smiling face changed to one of serious concern. They got to their feet and as they came closer, Tom could see all of Charles' clothes. "You are Charles Levi aren't you?" Tom asked.

"I am indeed Charles!" was the reply. "We don't have much time. I will explain later," He said in his memorable clear voice. "I have some items of great value for you to wear. You must put them on quickly." Charles tossed out two glowing bundles. Just like the mysterious craft, they never quite touched the ground but drifted an inch or so above the grass. The bundles were about a foot cubed and glowed with the same intensity of light as Charles' clothes did.

"You must act quickly and do exactly as I tell you. Your very lives are in danger! Open the bundles now!"

Tom and Sharon obediently dropped to their knees and reached for the bundles. They were so light in weight they could scarcely be felt. They began unfolding the bundles and separating the garments.

Charles said, "Your clothing will look just like mine. Quickly take up the belt and put it around your waist, then take up the breastplate to guard your heart, take up the shoes and put them on your feet. Now, take up the gold wristbands, which are your shields, and put them on your left wrists."

Sharon and Tom hurriedly did as they were commanded without really knowing why, but trusting Charles completely. He continued to guide them.

"Now, I give you your helmets. Place them firmly on your heads."

The helmets fit snugly but were so light they could scarcely be felt. Tom and Sharon noticed that all the garments were a perfect fit and conformed to the shape of their bodies. And they did indeed glow, just like Charles said they would.

"I give you your swords," Charles said ceremoniously as Tom and Sharon reached for the last remaining articles — cylinders, the size of an average flashlight.

"Aim your swords toward the sky and give a short squeeze."

They did as they were instructed and both were startled when brilliant blue bursts of light instantly discharged from the cylinders and arced across the sky as a bolt of lightning.

"Attach these to your belts then activate your shield by rubbing your right index finger across the gemstone on your gold wrist band."

Instantly, as the gemstones were touched, a panel of translucent material appeared in front of each of them. Each panel was two and a half feet wide and four feet tall. The center of the panel was attached to the wristband. Each panel consisted of rigid translucent material, extremely thin and very lightweight.

"That panel is a shield," Charles said. "Keep it between you and your enemy and it will protect you."

Tom said, "This plastic shield will protect us?"

"It is not plastic but it will protect you from any harm!" Charles replied. "All this clothing is your armor. It is indestructible. You are able to see this armor now as a visual reminder of its protection. There will soon come a time when you will no longer need to see it. Look around you. You will be able to see your enemy."

Tom and Sharon had been so intent as they put on their armor they had failed to notice that many other vehicles similar to Charles' had passed through the screen to the outside. The battle was no longer contained within the screen.

"But who is the enemy? Are all these the enemy?" Tom questioned.

"No they are not," Charles said. "Let me explain. When you look directly at the craft in the air, they all appear to be the same light color. We are in a battle with the forces of Satan. Just as he does in the lives of humans, he attempts to make his filthy schemes appear as good. Because of his deception all the craft appear to be pearly white. But, when you raise your shield of faith it will show you the truth. When you look through it, you will be able to discern that the evil ones are dark."

When they raised their shields, they could see that it was just as Charles said it would be. Some of the craft were dark when viewed through the shield and others like Charles's craft remained pearly white.

"So there's the enemy!"

"You learn quickly, my friends," Charles said softly. "Be alert! Don't be afraid! In the presence of danger always stand firm!" Charles motioned for them to step back. The craft accelerated skyward at an incredibly high rate of speed. It made no sound! In an instant it was a mile away and several hundred feet high. Soon they lost track of Charles among the other craft in the sky.

Through their shields Tom and Sharon watched uneasily as good battled evil, light against dark in an aerial display. The sky was filled with unbelievable mid-air maneuvers; high-speed chases, sudden stops, sharp turns. The machines defied natural law. Weapons discharged. Shafts of pure white light blasted from one craft to another. Energy beams and explosions packed the atmosphere.

Tom and Sharon were abruptly transformed from spectator to participant as they realized that the two of them were the targets of the enemy craft. The light craft had taken up defensive positions between them and the forces of darkness. Tom and Sharon's heavenly defenders deflected enemy beams fired in their direction. At any other time in their lives they would have been terrified at the thought of such dreadful power being used against them. But they had a sense of security as they watched the outnumbered light craft repel attack after attack. The dark craft suffered heavy losses each time they tried to break through. The enemy craft, damaged or destroyed, crashed into the meadow. The forces of evil were mighty, but were powerless to overcome the forces of good. Suddenly, an undeflected enemy beam was fired in Tom and Sharon's direction. When it struck the ground with a hateful vengeance a few yards away, Tom was instantly thankful that it missed them as the beam ripped up meadow grass and sod. That once familiar putrid odor filled the air. Absolute evil had scorched the earth at their feet.

In a mysterious but deliberate change of tactic, one dark craft suddenly turned and attacked another dark craft. This was a last ditch sinister effort to gain victory of killing either Tom or Sharon, even at the expense of killing one of its own.

"They're firing at their own guys?" Tom questioned to himself. "Why?"

The targeted craft exploded with violence upon being hit. A

large flaming piece of wreckage fell toward the ground, leaving a long trail of black smoke in its path. Tom watched with growing concern as the blazing fragment fell directly toward him and Sharon.

Above the din of the battle, Tom shouted, "Run! Sharon! Run!" as he pointed skyward. Each, without hesitation, ran toward open spaces in the meadow. To his utter dismay, Tom discovered that he and Sharon had run in opposite directions. Even worse, it was evident from the black smoke trail in the sky that the falling burning object had changed course in an ominous move and was still falling directly toward Sharon. Tom watched in wonder as Sharon's armor glowed brighter and brighter. He shouted a warning to her. Responding to his shout, she instantly recognized her ever-increasing danger. With a renewed burst of energy she bolted in a different direction. To Tom's complete disbelief the falling inferno once again changed course. As the danger grew nearer, Sharon's armor glowed brighter again. He watched helplessly as the instrument of Sharon's apparent destruction bore down on her. Time seemed to slow to a crawl. It was as if Sharon were moving in slow motion. In agony Tom carefully analyzed each second of time and every move she made. Exhausted from running, Sharon's pace slowed as she looked up. There was no escape. She came to a stop, planted her feet firmly and braced herself in defense. She raised the shield above her head and reached with her right hand for the handle of her sword. She pointed it skyward. Tom had drawn his sword. Simultaneously, they squeezed the handles and once again a lightning-type beam erupted from their swords, striking the falling, fiery object. Sharon's armor glowed with dazzling intensity. Tom watched in horror as the large flaming piece of wreckage crashed down and engulfed Sharon. It exploded into a massive orange and black rolling, boiling fireball. The ground quaked. Tom felt the searing heat of the impact as the acrid burnt odor assaulted his nostrils. He knew in his heart Sharon could not have survived. He had just watched the love of his life perish. His world and his future blurred before him as he anticipated an empty life without Sharon and the child they had never conceived. In utmost despair and with gut wrenching grief he collapsed to his knees. While gripping sod with each hand he pounded his helmeted head into the ground repeatedly as he screamed Sharon's name in anguish. Emotionally shattered, he sobbed bitterly. As he rose up, he pulled air into his lungs to fuel another scream. Tom choked in momentary disbelief as the impending scream turned into shouts of exhilaration. Through his tears, he saw Sharon running toward him from the flames. The light from her armor diminished as she distanced herself from the flaming wreckage. Pure exhilaration rushed into Tom's body to fill the void created by the grief from moments before. Tom leaped to his feet and ran eagerly to meet her. Waves of relief flooded his spirit. They held each other tightly in an ecstatic embrace, both shedding tears of sheer joy.

After holding and comforting Sharon for a while, Tom gently backed away and said, "Just let me look at you."

Sharon had just stepped out of a wall of fire, yet her body and clothing showed no hint of soot, neither did she have even the slightest smell of smoke. Her hair was tousled but not burned, not even singed. Miraculously there were no burns anywhere. Tom caressed his wife's face and thought this was the most beautiful he had ever seen her.

"Charles was right. I did what he said. I stood firm," Sharon whispered to Tom as he lovingly stroked her hair.

"I know you did. I saw."

Their armor glowed with a softer light. The battle was over. The wreckage of dark craft littered the ground. Victorious warriors busily carried their captives back into the screen. The clamor of battle that permeated the meadow moments before had faded away. One lone white craft settled gently and quietly toward the ground. Charles jumped from the craft to the ground, embraced the two of them and said: "Once again you have been delivered."

Sharon's adrenaline rush had subsided and physical weakness had begun to affect her. Charles' appearance had triggered a different emotional response in her. Tom steadied her as her body began to tremble. He tenderly stroked her ashen face. She spoke in broken sentences through her sobs, demanding answers from Charles.

"Come on aboard. There is much to discuss."

Charles led the way. A translucent dome sat atop the pearl white body of the craft. The dome covered the entire passenger compartment and extended to the floor at the rear. It appeared solid and had no door. Charles simply walked directly through the translucent material and took a seat inside. When Tom and Sharon hesitated Charles smiled and motioned for them to come on in. Tom tried to push on the dome with his finger. His finger simply passed through the material. Tom was startled and snatched his finger back.

Charles smiled at Tom's apprehension and said, "After all you've been through, now is not the time to doubt. Come in." Hesitantly, they walked through the apparent solid material. Instantly upon entering the craft a complete calmness washed over them.

"Have a seat," Charles said, as he gestured to benches molded into the sides of the craft. As Tom and Sharon positioned themselves, they were somewhat bewildered as they felt the benches move. The benches formed comfortable, soft seats as they conformed to an exact fit for the shapes of their bodies just as their armor had done. Since Tom and Sharon had entered the meadow, their senses had been flooded with impulses they had never experienced before. This was just one more of the unexplained.

They took mental inventory of the inside of the craft. They noted an absence of controls or instruments except for one gold panel that had four rows each containing three gemstones set in it. Each stone was different. All were astonishingly beautiful. A multi-faceted diamond sparkled with a rainbow of colors, an emerald of purest green, a sapphire of the richest royal blue, a ruby of brilliant red, and other gemstones they could not identify. Each of the 12 gemstones had a symbol or letter engraved in it and inlaid with gold. They didn't understand the meaning of the gold symbols. Neither did they take the time to ask.

Charles smiled and waited patiently while his visitors adjusted to their new surroundings.

Sharon said, "Charles, what did you mean when you said that we had been delivered once again? What is all this? What's going on? I don't understand what's happening! I'm afraid!"

"Don't be afraid. The one thing you need to understand now is that your lives are in danger. It is Satan's intention to kill you."

"Satan is trying to kill us?"

"Don't worry. He will not be allowed to hurt or kill either one of you. Satan can cause no harm that God doesn't allow. God's plan will be carried out in spite of Satan's best efforts. You see, today was not the first time an effort was made to take your lives."

Sharon remembered the only time she came near death was in an automobile accident several years earlier. "Are you talking about the car wreck I had?"

"Yes, the wreck was orchestrated by evil forces. You do recall the moments immediately before the crash."

"Yes," Sharon said. "I could never forget."

"You had the sensation that the car was not in your control."

"I do remember that feeling. I only told Tom about it, nobody else."

"You weren't in control! Evil forces caused the wreck. The car flipped end over end, and yet your life was spared. You walked away without a scratch."

"Oh!" Sharon replied as she gripped Tom's arm tighter.

"And, Tom, you too have not gone unnoticed. Do you remember that cold day when you were a kid, you stood too close to a campfire and your clothes caught fire?"

"I do! I was scared to death!"

"Well that was the first attempt. The next was during the Second Gulf War."

"That mine explosion was planned?" Tom gulped.

"Yes, Satan has determined plans to eliminate you."

"But it was my decision to stop the Humvee and get out."

"But who gave you the idea, Tom?"

"I see…" Tom's voice trailed off.

"The other time was right across the road in the ditch filled with water."

"Do you mean that was a deliberate attempt to kill me too?"

"Precisely! But that's not all," Charles reported. "There was another attempt made on Sharon's life."

"There was?"

"Yes, the place you call the climbing tree."

Sharon's face grew pale. She felt an icy coldness as she remembered that childhood day when she fell from her favorite tree. She was only shaken, but always since that day the tree had seemed evil and menacing.

"If there weren't forces in place to protect you, a broken neck would have ended your life that day."

For a moment all the related incidents were as fresh as if they had happened yesterday as Tom and Sharon recalled them in vivid detail. They were overwhelmed with the knowledge that they had been saved from certain death.

Charles continued, "And then there were the events of today. You see, you have been drawn to this time and place to help fulfill a special plan. It is Satan's intention to subvert the plan."

"What plan?"

"God has a great plan. Satan has attempted to kill one or both of you in order to prevent the birth of a child – a child that will grow up to be a mighty man of God. God's plan is for you to have a son."

Sharon laughed. "The doctors have said that having a baby is impossible for us."

"With God, nothing is impossible!"

Sharon spoke nervously for fear of offending Charles. Her voice wavered. "You have told us so many incredible things, Charles. I must ask you. How can we know what you say is true?"

Charles said not a word. He simply smiled, reached to the panel of gemstones, and waved his hand. Then he looked back at Tom and Sharon's faces as they reacted to the first melodious notes of Sleepwalk.

"It's you! You're the one!" Sharon cried out.

"You're the guitar player from our senior prom! You played that song just for us! You knew our names!" Tom exclaimed.

"Proof enough!" Sharon said.

"Yes, proof enough!" Tom added.

CHAPTER 14

To Tom and Sharon the opportunity to sit in Charles' craft, to observe its unadorned and simple design and listen to Charles' voice was a unique experience. The neophytes in Charles' presence were mentally formulating questions. "How could he be the guitar player at their senior prom, since he hadn't aged? Where did he come from? How did he get here? What is Charles' role in the events of the last several days? What was actually happening?"

Before any of these heavy questions could be asked, Charles interjected some light discussion. He related to Tom once again how much he enjoyed the ride the two of them had taken over Roller Coaster Hills. Tom knew that riding in the T-bird could be thrilling, but Charles seemed to be extraordinarily impressed by the experience.

"Allow me to treat you to a ride in my equivalent of your T-bird." Charles said. His anticipation was one of high expectation. It was much like Tom's expression that day as he had expectantly waited for Charles to turn the ignition switch to start the T-bird's engine. To Sharon it was apparent that men of all ages could still be boys.

Charles swiveled in his wrap-around captain's seat mounted front center in the craft. "Permit me to demonstrate for you." Charles said as he touched the gemstones on the gold panel.

Sharon's attention was drawn to the beauty of the exquisite gemstones. She noticed that one of the gemstones on the panel matched exactly the stones on their wristbands. Charles' gemstone was pure white and matched none of those on the panel. Before Sharon could even formulate the question in her mind, Charles answered, "The stones are identical to the ones worn on the breast-plate of the High Priest. They each represent one of the 12 tribes of Israel."

When Charles' fingers left the panel, the craft left the earth. The scenery outside the dome sped by in a maddening blur, giving a visual sensation of tremendous speed. They felt none of the physical discomforts associated with such an unexpected rate of acceleration. While Tom and Sharon sat comfortably in their seats, their minds recognized the high altitude but they could not comprehend the speed. The impact of the unusual visual sensations had not fully registered. Charles waited with expectation.

The sensation was similar to that experienced at amusement park theaters with screens that completely surround the audience. While the participants sit safely in their seats, the movements in the screen excite the visual cortex to its limits. Tom and Sharon had experienced virtual reality before. What Charles was showing them was not virtual, it was real.

Tom was the first to break the silence with, "Uh, Charles, how did - uh- did you – I mean, how did you do that?"

Charles didn't contain himself any longer. He threw back his head and laughed from the depths of his being. "To put it in drag strip vernacular, you have just gone from zero to twenty thousand miles per hour in 1.2 seconds." He waited for his words to register.

In wondrous amazement, Tom's first comment was, "Wow!"

After a moment's thought, he asked, "But what about G-forces, laws of inertia and all that I've studied in physics. How did we even survive the take-off? Why didn't we feel the movement?" His perplexed voice revealed his confusion.

Charles chuckled again. His light-heartedness was contagious. Tom and Sharon were becoming amused at their own bewilderment. It was as if they had been told a funny joke and everyone got the punch line except the two of them.

"Let me explain." Charles began, "Do you remember our discussion concerning the bacteria on the New Jersey beach? And how it would be easier for someone to explain the politics of Brazil to bacteria, than for man to understand God? Bacteria cannot possibly understand politics. Man cannot fully understand the power of God. Your limitations keep you from understanding.

"The principle applies here as well. You see, the Lord God of all creation created nature and nature's laws. It appears to you that those laws have been violated. That is not the case. People rarely witness some of God's laws. You can read in your Bible, the record that has been left for you, that the Spirit transported the apostle Philip suddenly out of the desert. The laws that govern travel at the speeds you have just experienced require a high degree of faith. Through faith, you can move mountains, walk on water and throw a tree into the sea. The Lord God will honor His promises that all things are possible through Him. Soon you will have an opportunity to fully exercise the faith you have been given to receive those promises. There will come a time that another great covenant promise will be fulfilled. One day you, along with many others, will know and understand everything in all of creation and in heaven itself." Neither Tom nor Sharon pressed Charles further. They were learning to accept everything he said as truth. They had not tested his words and deeds for accuracy to find him honest and true. They were supernaturally given an understanding that they were to trust this man in all things. They listened.

"As you look down you will notice that we are traveling at a high rate of speed. Even from this altitude of 35,000 feet, we can watch the landscape go by quickly."

Charles smiled as he watched startled expressions form on his guests' faces.

"Yes," he went on, "at this speed we could go around the whole world in just a little bit over an hour. If an observer on the ground were watching us we would appear to be traveling across the sky at approximately the speed of the meteors we saw a few nights ago when we were watching that incredible meteor display at the lake."

Tom and Sharon understood the concept very well. They were fascinated and eager to hear more.

"I will now demonstrate my version of your Roller Coaster Hills!" Charles said with a playful grin. "Watch the position of the sun."

The obedient students did as Charles asked. Suddenly, the sun changed direction from straight ahead to a position on their left.

Once again Charles waited for a response and once again he was presented with speechless, questioning faces.

Before either of them stuttered broken questions Charles responded, "We were traveling due east with the morning sun in our faces. We are now traveling due south with the sun to our left. We made a 90-degree turn at nearly twenty thousand miles per hour in one half second flat! How's that for performance?"

It suddenly occurred to Charles' passengers that they had been making radical high speed turns all along. They had seen the sun from all four directions during their short flight. They had been traveling in a great circle. But in their excitement they had not assessed the significance of those events. Even if they were mentally comparable to bacteria, the new information they possessed was thrilling.

"What about G-forces?" Tom questioned. "Charles, I don't understand!"

"Remember the bacteria?" Charles reminded. "One of the greatest thrills during the drive in your car was feeling the G-forces. Gaining weight from centrifugal force as we went into the dips in the road is a sensation that I cannot experience with our mode of travel. I felt that sensation as the car went over the hilltops. The sensation I experienced was utterly amazing when the wheels left the pavement and the lap belts tugged at our bodies. Rounding the curves was yet another. That ride was as exhilarating to me as this is to you. This is an everyday thing to me. The ride in your car was not."

Charles slowed the craft to 300 mph and descended to an altitude of 5,000 feet. As they passed over Cincinnati, they turned due north. They cruised over rolling hills and fields and meadows dotted with ponds and lakes. Fences created checkerboards of various shades of green pasture and plowed ground. Suddenly there appeared memorable landscape ahead — the cabin, and the lake. Charles eased the craft to a hovering speed so the beauty of the place could be savored. The passengers looked down on the lake and the familiar cabin beside it. They noticed the Pritchards sitting in their lawn chairs at the water's edge.

"That really is their favorite spot," Sharon commented as they flew directly overhead.

"Charles," Tom asked, "why is no one looking up as we go over?"

"They can't see us," was the reply. "Sometimes people can see the rippling of leaves in the tops of trees as the craft passes through. Most people think it's just the wind. Only those who are permitted can see."

"What do you mean permitted? Never mind, I'm still bacteria!" Tom laughed.

They slowly passed over the cabin and lake area. This bird's eye view of the smorgasbord of flowers behind the cabin was a rolling carpet of color all the way to the woods. The craft nearly touched the treetops. The leaves on the tops of the trees rippled as they were churned in the wake of the craft.

"I think we had better start back," Charles announced as he turned the craft toward the west.

Eager eyes watched as Charles' fingers gently touched the gemstones. The craft responded to his commands and increased speed to 300 mph once again. Tom's mind buzzed with a thousand questions concerning the physics that allowed the craft to perform, but he knew by now that he would not understand the answers.

Sharon, however, had no interest in the physics of flight. The unique upholstery of the craft piqued her curiosity. She moved to the bench on the other side of the craft and sat down. Just as before the bench instantly became a custom fit seat. She made an attempt to identify the lavish fabric. It was ivory in color, immaculate in design without a blemish anywhere, soft as premium cashmere and as delicate as a down-filled pillow of the finest quality. She pushed and molded the fibers and when she released her hand the cushions instantly sprang back to original form. As she continued to finger the fabric of the seats, she again noticed and further contemplated her gold wristband with its single stone. Her stone matched exactly one of the gemstones on the gold panel in front of Charles.

Charles made a pass over Wright Patterson Air Force Base in Dayton. He saw that the U.S. Air Force Museum was directly below. Vintage aircraft of all types were displayed both inside and outside the hangers.

Charles' craft gained altitude as they flew directly west. Soon the tall buildings of downtown Indianapolis appeared on the horizon. At a distance of seventy miles the buildings looked like black pencils standing on their erasers silhouetted against the brilliantly clear sky. Tom and Sharon had never seen the air so pristine. If they had asked why, Charles would have told them that the dome covering the craft screened out impurities in the air like a polarizing filter, causing the air to appear crystal clear.

Charles swiveled in his chair to face his passengers, "Look at that!" he called out.

Approaching from behind and on each side of the craft were two F-16s with missiles mounted under their wings. The aircraft matched Charles' speed as they pulled alongside. The pilots surveyed them with much interest. The fighter on the left suddenly pulled ahead and took up a position directly in front of and above the craft. From inside the craft their view was the underside of the F-16. The fighter on the right was so close Tom could count the rivets on its smooth skin.

"What are they doing?" Sharon asked in a nervous tone.

"Just watch," Charles replied. "This could be fun."

As they watched, the fighter on the right extended its landing gear. The pilot pointed down with his finger and jabbed his hand up and down in a gesturing fashion. He retracted his landing gear then quickly repeated the procedure.

"He wants to look at our wheels?" Sharon asked naively.

Tom burst out in laughter. Charles grinned.

"What???" Sharon asked in an exasperated tone. She looked first at Charles, then at Tom for an answer.

Through his chuckles Tom explained that the fighter pilot was demanding that they land their craft.

"Anyway," Charles added, "we don't even have wheels."

Sharon responded with a very weak, "Oh..." feeling a bit embarrassed.

"They're about to make their move," Charles announced.

They watched as the F-16 on the right crowded in closer and the one above and in front began a descent. Its reduction in altitude put it closer and closer to the nose of the craft. To avoid a collision it was necessary for Charles to make a slow descending turn to the left.

"Looks like they want us to go back to Wright Patterson," Tom said.

"They do indeed!" Charles replied. "But watch what happens!"

Charles touched the gemstones on the gold panel once more and the craft instantly dropped a hundred feet and accelerated to a tremendous rate of speed, traveled a short distance, and turned again to the west. In no time at all they were slowing their speed as they approached the meadow.

"I think those F-16 pilots just saw a UFO," Tom said jokingly.

"Yes, they did," Charles said. "They were allowed to see an unidentified craft, it was flying, and it was an object. So yes, they did technically see a UFO. Their problem is, though, they will not remember."

"Do you mean they won't remember anything at all?"

"No, they had some excitement for a few minutes, but they will not be permitted to retain any memory of those events. The time is not right for them. Not yet anyway." Charles lowered the craft to a soft landing in the meadow.

Wreckage that was strewn about in the meadow had been removed. There were no remnants remaining of the fierce battle between good and evil.

With reflective expectation, Tom and Sharon waited. After a moment, Charles spoke tenderly, "To answer your question from earlier, yes, I am the guitar player. I have watched over you unseen all your lives. In the Iraq desert, I was there; when the car was wrecked, I took control; at the campfire, I quenched the flames; at the climbing tree, I cushioned Sharon's fall. And today, it was you, more mature in your faith, who stood firm. Now you are ready."

While Charles was still speaking, a sense of understanding and acceptance washed over them both. On the dance floor that night so many years earlier, when Tom and Sharon's eyes met, their souls meshed and they knew that together a new life had begun. Charles' words evoked an identical emotion in each of them. And so...they listened...with receptive hearts, as Charles continued.

"In ages past, even before the earth was created, a plan was established. It was a magnificent plan – the plan for human redemption, prophesied and fulfilled. Other prophecies are yet to be realized. You can share in the completion of one of those prophecies. The tribes of Israel shall assemble together. A certain number of them will be set aside for spiritual purity. They will be **sealed for a purpose**. They will be protected from spiritual harm and will be secured in their destiny. You have been drawn to this time and place for a reason. Because of your ancestry one of your descendants can be one of those who are sealed."

"Ancestry? I thought the people of Israel were Jews. We are not Jewish, so how can this be?"

"Today the descendents of Israel and the name Jews have become synonymous. The Jews are not the full House of Israel; they come from one tribe, the tribe of Judah, which includes the tiny tribe of Benjamin. Long ago the ten tribes in the northern kingdom of Israel were scattered into all parts of the world. Their national and tribal identity was absolutely destroyed, just as God the Father said it would be. The obliteration of their identity was so complete that even they don't know who they are. One reason why the tribe of Judah has remained distinct in its identity is so there could be no mistake from which tribe the Messiah descended. It had to be the tribe of Judah to fulfill the prophecy that the Messiah would be a Jew. It is impossible for persons worldwide to trace their tribal lineage except that they are given divine understanding, as I am about to give you. You are both descendents of the patriarch Joseph. Joseph's right to inherit the tribal blessing was divided into two parts and given to his two sons, Ephraim and Manasseh. Your ancestry comes through Joseph's son Manasseh. Therefore, you are descendents of the tribe of Manasseh."

"This son you say we will have, will he be one of those who are sealed?"

"He may be, or he may be a parent, or grandparent, or great-grandparent or so on. We don't know when this assembly of that prophesied group will be called together. Only God the Father knows the time. It is our concern to always be prepared to act when called."

Sharon listened to all that Charles said, trying to put the pieces of the mystery together. She did not want to misunderstand. "You're saying we have been chosen and no matter what we do we will be guided to fulfill that prophecy? Does that mean we don't have a choice?"

"You are drawn to the point of choice. The choice you have to make is simple. Do you believe that with God all things are possible? If you believe, you will be given a son and will receive fulfillment beyond anything you can imagine. If you do not fully exercise your gift of faith, others will take your places who also qualify in the chain of kinship. You see, the fulfillment of the prophecy will be carried out with or without you, just as it was with Ruth and Boaz. They were brought together to fulfill a prophecy. They were unaware that they would have a great grandson who would be the great King David of Israel. Nor were they aware that they would be ancestors of the Messiah himself. The choice was theirs. The choice is yours."

"How do we choose?"

"You will know when the time comes. The Father already knows. He knows you as well as He knows that sparrow behind you." Tom and Sharon turned to see a sparrow suspended in the midst of its full flight 15 feet away. It was absolutely motionless in the air. For the first time since the screen appeared, they became aware that everything earthly in and around the meadow was immobile. It was difficult for their minds to comprehend what their eyes saw. Nothing moved. Helicopter rotors were frozen. Soldiers were locked in place. The air was perfectly still. Tree leaves were unmoving. No grass stirred below the helicopters as they hung in mid-air. Steve and his family were rigidly set in place. Not even a stray hair moved on their heads. The sheriff's deputies, fixed in full stride, were like statues. J.T. was still suspended above the ground after having jumped for joy when he captured the medallion.

With Charles leading, they all stepped out of the craft. Charles walked over to J.T., took the gold medallion out of his hands, then turned and said, "All these people who think the medallion is a key to the dimensional shift port are sadly mistaken. It's only a piece of jewelry. It's like most everything else that you have seen and experienced here. It is an illusion to help you understand spiritual warfare."

"You mean it didn't really happen?"

"Oh, yes, it happened, but it happened in the spirit dimension as time stood still on earth."

There was a moment of silence as Tom and Sharon considered Charles' words. They listened attentively as he continued.

"Just as Adam and Eve were a vital part of the beginning, the two of you and your descendents are a vital part of the end."

Slowly and thoughtfully Sharon questioned, "Charles, I have to ask... are... you... an... angel?" Sharon questioned.

"Very perceptive of you, Sharon," Charles responded. "I will share this much with you. I made my choice in ancient times to serve the Most High God. I, along with many others, helped defend heaven against those who turned to evil. Now, at the direction of Gabriel and the great archangel Michael, I minister to the redeemed. My job is to guide, protect, and encourage people such as the two of you. You are well on your way to becoming mature in the faith. You are strengthening your spiritual gifts. Soon you will be flooded with understanding. It seems my work with you is nearly complete, but it is with greatly anticipated joy that we in the heavenly realm await the day the redeemed come home," Charles continued. "The two of you have heard the knock. You have opened the door. You have allowed the Redeemer to enter. You have made that choice. Will you make the choice to believe that with God all things are possible? Will you accept the responsibility to parent a great man of God – your son?"

As Charles boarded the craft, he turned to them and said, "I have delivered the message. I must leave you now."

"Charles, will we see you again?"

"In your lifetime you will see me working with others who are but spiritual children in the faith."

"Will we remember any of this?" Sharon asked.

"You will remember nothing of the illusion that you were permitted to see today until the proper time, but, to keep you on course, there will be markers along the way. Watch the trees. Pay attention and watch. Some call it deja vu."

Charles took his seat and in an instant traveled into the screen.

CRAAACK! The screen vanished.

With nerve-shattering suddenness, the entire meadow exploded back to life. The formerly frozen helicopters roared with powerful vibration. The grass beneath them was beaten violently by great blasts of air from the helicopters' rotor wash. Soldiers' shouts were heard in the yells of confusion while they searched for creatures that were now invisible to their sophisticated equipment. Sheriff's deputies wrestled J.T. to the ground. They secured him with handcuffs.

"The medallion, the medallion!" J.T. cried. "You guys stole my medallion!"

The deputies protested that they stole nothing as they escorted an angry, resisting J.T. to the police car and placed him firmly in the back seat. As the helicopters settled to the ground, the soldiers searched meticulously with no success for the two mysterious creatures.

Tom retrieved a camera from the truck. He criss-crossed the meadow, taking pictures of the events from all possible angles. "This will make tremendous copy for the paper," he said aloud as he shot roll after roll of film.

The sheriff jailed J.T. and impounded his car. The military men in the meadow were radioed from headquarters to cease their investigation and evacuate the area. The response was immediate. As suddenly as they appeared, the helicopters vanished. An eerie quiet settled over the meadow. The pulsing turmoil of a few moments earlier was replaced by the tranquility and calm of a normal summer morning.

As they excitedly gathered on top of the hill at Arlin's house, the three families recounted the amazing events of the early morning intrusion into their peaceful surroundings. Tom and Arlin, with their cameras, had documented the event well. Arlin hurried to the VCR to rewind the cassette from his video camera. The inquisitive friends intently watched the replay of the morning's events. The video began with J.T. standing at his car, looking through binoculars toward the woods. As J.T. walked into the meadow, Arlin turned his camera to record the arrival of the two Blackhawk helicopters and the unloading of the troops. He recorded the appearance of the sheriff's deputies just before Tom and Sharon came through the gate. The camera recorded J.T. as he continued walking, ignoring the new arrivals. Steve and his family hurried through the gate and stopped beside Tom's truck. All the people watching the videotape had been eyewitnesses as the two creatures appeared and then mysteriously disappeared. They waited expectantly to see what the videotape would reveal. For an instant, a dazzling flash of light was the only unusual event on the tape. The gray creatures simply vanished in the flash as the deputies approached J.T. to arrest him. While watching the tape Tom and Sharon experienced something like a vacant memory…just out of reach. The others felt as if they had looked away from a TV program just as the key to the mystery was given.

The group replayed the tape many times. Slow motion, stop action, and frame-by-frame analysis of the flash of light revealed only…a flash…of light.

CHAPTER 15

+≡≡+

DIEGO GARCIA, INDIAN OCEAN

To most people, Diego Garcia is an almost unnoticeable dot on a map near the middle of the Indian Ocean. To veteran military planners, Diego Garcia is a very important military asset to Britain and the United States. A group of islands, Diego Garcia has been referred to as the equivalent of a giant stationary aircraft carrier. The airbase complex is the home base of a number of B-52s, air refueling tankers, fighter squadrons, and reconnaissance aircraft, including the U-2 and SR-71 Blackbird.

In a somewhat secluded area of one runway complex waited a squadron of U.S. Navy P-3 Orion antisubmarine aircraft. The aircraft were unarmed. Their only defense was a somewhat limited array of counter measure devices. These sleek, gleaming white aircraft hunted down submarines from nations the world over. During the Cold War, when the Soviets wanted to know where their own subs were, they simply located the operational areas of the P-3 Orions. As if by magic, the Soviet subs would be nearby. Of all the U.S. Navy's Orion squadrons, the one stationed at Diego Garcia was rated the very best. Its professionalism and excellence in submarine location was the envy of all other Orion squadrons. The aircraft nicknamed Dragonfly was, without question, the best of the best!

The Dragonfly's senior officer and pilot was Commander Ray Bishop, a graduate of the U.S. Naval Academy. Her first officer was

Lt. Commander Carl Jones, and the tactical coordinator was Lt. Commander Josh Evans. Jones and Evans were Naval ROTC graduates. All three men were U.S. Navy professionals. The rest of the crew consisted of ten enlisted men, each expertly cross-trained in specialized areas of submarine hunting techniques. Among other P-3 Orion squadrons, these men had no equal in the areas of reconnaissance collection, high-speed still frame photography and video, radio interception, data transmission, electronic warfare counter measures, and telemetry interpretation.

The telemetry interpreter was the newest member of the Dragonfly crew, Antisubmarine Warfare Technician First Class, better known as A W 1 Richard Franklin. His job was to intercept and interpret telemetry of any kind from a targeted submarine. Mr. Franklin was a uniquely talented young man and was sought after by many aircraft commanders. He had one exceptionally notable characteristic, a constant smile on his face. He had been expertly trained in operation of the Navy's new device, a very low frequency underwater radio transmission detector. This technology allowed submarines to communicate around the world while submerged by using radio frequencies which ranged from three to thirty kHz; 3,000 to 30,000 cycles per second. Very low frequency radio transmissions use the ocean for their antennae. The difficulty was intercepting the signal. Part of Mr. Franklin's job was to intercept and interpret submarines' communications as well as monitor any other electronic transmissions a submarine might be emitting. He could read the heartbeat of the submarine. The U.S. Navy had the equipment. Mr. Franklin had the talent. The Dragonfly had Mr. Franklin.

There was another and most unusual attribute of the Dragonfly. Each crewman was hand picked by Commander Bishop. He selected the men, not only for their superior job performance, but for their high moral character as well.

The Dragonfly crew mingled very little with other crews. They formed a close-knit and serious fraternity. The crew stayed quietly secluded in their barracks, studying ancient manuscripts of Judeo-Christian heritage when they weren't on missions. Because of this self-imposed isolation, others viewed them as being somewhat odd.

Adding to the mystery surrounding the crew itself was one of the two insignia painted on the aircraft. Just under the pilot's window in the usual place on the fuselage was the pilot's rank and name. Just below the pilot's name were two paintings, each about three feet square. On the left was a painting of a colorful dragonfly, clearly appropriate due to the nature of the hunt, with the word Dragonfly lettered in semicircular fashion underneath the painting. A real mystery surrounded the painting immediately to the right, an impressive depiction of an antiquated stemmed gray cup with handles on either side. It was superimposed upon a maroon shield background. Its semi-circular name read, "Order of the Holy Grail", which was the final touch to seal the mystery. The paintings were repeated on the opposite side of the aircraft under the first officer's window. The other P-3 Orion crews buzzed from time to time about what "Order of the Holy Grail" meant; on this matter the Dragonfly's crew was strangely silent.

CHAPTER 16

W hile viewing the videotape with the others, Tom furiously penned notes. After meticulous examination there was no video data to determine what had become of the unidentified creatures. They had simply disappeared in the mysterious flash of light.

The fact was, the two stranded creatures had finally returned into their rightful realm. The people viewing the tape were oblivious to that detail. Also they were unaware that several hours had been compressed into a brief one and one half seconds. During that flicker of time a spiritual battle had been fought and a journey had been taken in a most unusual aircraft from an Indiana meadow to a lakeside cabin in western Ohio.

Tom had much writing to do. His true, investigative reporting skills that lay dormant for years were now pressed into service.

Tom spent the rest of that day interviewing his neighbors. Each person had a different point of view and potential explanation. Some even suggested space/time dimension shifts. He assembled their eyewitness accounts along with their theories, attempting to formulate complete clarification. Their stories in Tom's hands merged to form a masterfully detailed picture of the week's events. The newspaper publisher switched to high-speed production as the presses ran on into the night and up into the next day…and the day after…and the day after that. Sales quickly outstripped production. Updated editions followed as quickly as they could be printed. The photo department logged hours of overtime. Business was robust throughout the summer. The editorial page was expanded to include response columns where bona fide and quasi-scientific explanations were presented and argued. Everyone it seemed had an opinion or theory. No new facts emerged.

Sam, healthy and rested, came back to work. He was pleased at the increased production; he was reminded of the old days when he worked for a bustling daily newspaper. The Hoosier Tribune received orders for bundles of newspapers from other states and from as far away as Canada and England. Although the full stories and pictures were available on the internet, people still wanted souvenir newspapers.

It appeared the whole world wanted to know what happened to the two unidentified, possibly extraterrestrial, gray creatures in a meadow in central Indiana. Tom's articles infused into a small weekly newspaper new life. A sleepy little newspaper awakened. The Hoosier Tribune was back in the "real" news business.

CHAPTER 17

3:32 AM LOCAL TIME AUGUST 19
DIEGO GARCIA, INDIAN OCEAN

Her powerful landing lights sliced through the pre-dawn darkness as the Dragonfly traveled down the taxiway. Off to the right, the dim runway marker lights cast an eerie bluish glow in the fine, foggy mist that hovered a few feet above the ground. The Dragonfly's wings rocked up and down as her wheels rolled over small dips and rises in the taxiway pavement. As she traveled toward the runway, it felt to the crew as if they were riding a goose as she waddled ungracefully along.

The first officer and crew were putting the finishing touches on the preflight checklist. Commander Bishop brought the Dragonfly to a stop just short of the runway. Takeoff permission and flight instructions were requested, as per routine, from the tower.

"Dragonfly, you are cleared for takeoff on runway two one right. Proceed outbound at zero two one degrees, to angels five, then vector two niner six to angels one five. Proceed to your patrol zone. Your patrol zone Skyboss is Eagle's Roost." Then after a pause, "Good hunting, sir. Over."

"Roger, tower, thanks. Over," came Commander Bishop's reply as he repeated his flight instructions.

Tower operators who dealt with the Dragonfly noticed that there was always a short delay before she pulled onto the runway after receiving instructions. It always happened with the Dragonfly. It was somewhat unusual for such an aircraft. No one questioned the practice. They just noticed. Only the Dragonfly's crew knew that the sixty-second delay was written into the pre-takeoff checklist. In that sixty seconds Commander Bishop led the crew in asking God's blessing for a successful mission.

Right on schedule, a short burst of power from the engines rolled the Dragonfly slowly onto the end of the runway. She swung around to put her nose wheels squarely in the center of giant numbers painted on the concrete. They read 21R.

Commander Bishop locked the brakes as the flaps were lowered. His right hand advanced the throttles as the four turbo prop engines revved to ninety percent of rated power. The flight engineer watched the instruments closely as each engine's rpm steadied. The pilot released the brakes and the Dragonfly lunged forward into the night. Faster and faster she accelerated. Vibrations from the propellers permeated the entire aircraft. Soon the Dragonfly was at lift off speed but she stayed on the runway.

The first officer watched the instruments and called off airspeed and runway distance markers to Commander Bishop.

"Point of no return mark coming up in ten seconds, sir...no return in five...four...three...two...one. We are committed to flight, sir."

Commander Bishop and his first officer worked with practiced precision. As Bishop pulled back on the yoke, the spinning tires lost contact with the pavement. The first officer instantly pulled in the landing gear and closed the bay doors. The Dragonfly climbed quickly. The flaps were pulled in. At five thousand feet she made her turn to two nine six degrees and continued to climb to fifteen thousand feet. Commander Bishop throttled back to cruising speed. He trimmed the aircraft and engaged the autopilot. The Dragonfly continued through the dark sky toward her patrol zone.

For the moment Dragonfly was alone among the stars.

CHAPTER 18

+≍=≍+

9:30 AM AUGUST 18 INDIANAPOLIS, INDIANA

After a tiring but exhilarating eight weeks, Tom was presented with a huge bonus by Hoosier Tribune management. In addition they ordered him to take a well-deserved vacation. There were loose ends that required attention, however. Colonel William Keller returned to Indianapolis, along with his staff, to conduct in-depth interviews. A new national investigation was launched.

During the investigation Colonel Keller remembered that day in his dad's hospital room when he encountered Tom Alexander. He regretted not having pressed Tom for more information. Colonel Keller was a "by the book" air force officer. He followed procedure to the letter. By not skirting certain classified issues with Tom he had deprived himself of information that could have made him an eyewitness to the events in the meadow. Colonel Keller was not a man to live by regrets. The investigation continued.

Tom and Sharon picked up the repaired T-bird and with a flip of a coin their new adventure began. Successive flips of the coin placed the T-bird on highways leading to the foothills of the Great Smoky Mountains National Park, driving south on I-75 through Kentucky and Tennessee.

As they passed through each cut in the mountain ridges, they saw more confirmation that a powerful hand was at work in creation. To build smooth roadbeds highway construction crews had sliced through steep mountain ridges, exposing sections of sedimentary rock layers. Layers that would normally lay flat were nearly standing on their ends. Steep angles of the layers illustrated that many catastrophic events had taken place in the formation of earth. Tom and Sharon soaked in the geological beauty of the mountains, marveling at how the hand of man had exposed God's handiwork.

On they traveled through mountainous curves as the sun warmed their wind blown faces while the radio crackled with disturbing news.

> ..."*Abrams Report disclosed early this morning information it discovered through private channels that military action on at least two fronts by China is imminent. Red Chinese army alert has been heightened to unprecedented scale. Intercepted coded communications are in an almost frenzied state. Exactly what the Chinese Communist intentions are is unclear. However, the Chinese are enabling the Iranians to attack Israel. Three days ago the Russian-built and Chinese armed submarine, bow number 504, abruptly left its Iranian port. It left under cover of darkness and submerged before daybreak. It is known that the submarine is carrying Chinese made medium range nuclear missiles. Israel, Japan, South Korea, and Taiwan have all, through diplomatic channels, reminded the United States of their promise to assist militarily if any one of these countries is attacked. The United States and Taiwan have not had official diplomatic relations since 1979 but the long-standing defense agreement that they made at that time has never been withdrawn. Also Pentagon officials stated today that they feared a submarine missile attack by the Iranians against Israel. What I hold right here in my fingers could be the most explosive announcement since the initial bulletins about the attack on Pearl Harbor. Have the Muslims expanded their war of terrorism*

to include the use of nuclear missiles? As you well know the Abrams Report has an accuracy rating surpassed by none. If they say that the Red Chinese army is engaging in these activities, you can depend on it..."

The radio talk show host rattled the papers in the microphone to make his point but his tone was somber as he proclaimed his warning. The radio station faded out before Tom and Sharon heard the host's last comment, "...people, I am telling you, prepare for WAR!" Their attention turned instead to the natural beauty surrounding them.

The mountain air carried the fresh scent of pine as they drove. Having the top down on the convertible allowed Tom and Sharon to enjoy the heady effect of the many aromas. They threaded their way through great leafy tunnels formed by massive maples that arched their branches over the winding road.

They drove up a high hill that overlooked a town spread throughout the valley below. Tom was thankful to see a gas station at the very top of the hill. The timing was very nearly perfect. The gas gauge had just bumped empty.

Tom parked at the pumps and turned the ignition off. He and Sharon slowly climbed out of the low-slung car. Riding in the small car was a thrill, but after a couple of hours, they each developed a keen desire to stand up and stretch their aching limbs. They moved about in an attempt to recover their mobility.

Tom placed the nozzle in the tank while Sharon thoughtfully observed the beauty of the mountains in the distance. Tom looked up to see her glowing smile change to an expression of sadness. In mere seconds tears welled in her eyes as she looked right past him. Tom turned to see what had affected her so dramatically.

Across the street stood an old dilapidated building – or at least for the moment it still stood. A demolition crew was in the process of tearing it down. The building was an old church that had been converted to a mission of sorts. A crane sat at the front door, its boom raised high into the air. A cable ran from the boom to a massive sign that was being removed from high atop the roof. It was a huge cross with big neon letters which read, "Jesus Saves."

The cable was wrapped around the horizontal beam of the cross. They watched as the crane lifted the sign off the roof. As it was lowered, workers guided the cross into a waiting dump truck parked at the corner of the building.

When the cross shifted as it settled into the steel truck bed, the glass tubes of the neon letters crushed. Escaping gas from the broken tubes produced puffs of white clouds. Glass crunched. Sharp shards ricocheted, as they struck steel. The truck rocked back and forth as the crane operator maneuvered and adjusted the cross, lowering it into its final position. Glass continued to break with each movement. After the last adjustment the cable was removed. The lingering sound was a high-pitched tinkle and the jingle of tiny pieces of glass coming to rest. The services of the sign were no longer required.

Without fanfare the truck moved away from the building toward the street. The cross lay in the truck bed at an angle. One crossbar protruded into the air while the top of the cross extended out above the cab of the truck. Several people stood with saddened faces watching as the truck rattled out across the sidewalk and into the street.

"I know that old buildings sometimes need to be torn down and old crosses have to be removed too. It seems so sad to watch," Sharon lamented as she sat back down in the car and wiped her tears.

Tom finished filling the tank and went inside to pay his bill. The cashier had watched the same scene through the window. He too had a saddened expression.

"It's a shame they have to tear the building down," Tom said as he paid the gas bill.

"It's the end of an age," came the cashier's reply. "That old mission has been here for as long as I can remember. The cross has lit up the night sky like a lighthouse beacon every night. Up here on this hill it could be seen from most any place in town. People saw that cross in the dark of night and knew that they could get comfort and aid any time from the old man who ran the place."

"Was that place a kind of rescue mission?" Tom asked.

"Well, it was a lot more than that to many people, me included," the cashier said thoughtfully. "For me, the old man and the mission meant the difference between finding salvation and being spiritually lost. He showed me a new life and then he got me this job. Everything changed for me. The lowest of the low were drawn by the light of that cross. We left our problems and found real happiness...no, not just happiness - it was real joy on this hill."

"Who is the old man?" Tom inquired.

"The Old Man, that's what he wanted everybody to call him. He bought the old church from donations he collected and turned it into a mission. He made it a safe place for all who would come. The mission was not up to meetin' building codes so the city ordered it torn down. They said they were afraid it would catch fire or somethin'. The old man died last week. At least they had the decency to wait until he passed to tear it down. It would've killed him sooner if he had seen that cross come down today. All he ever wanted was for that sign on top to draw more people in."

"We had a meeting in the mission last night," the cashier went on, "sort of a tribute to The Old Man. Every one of us had a special story to tell about how our lives were changed. You know, mister, I do believe that the light moved from that sign up on the roof to inside the mission last night. It seemed that the whole place glowed really bright as all the stories were told."

Tears were streaming down the cashier's face, his lips quivered and his voice made no more sound.

If Tom could have seen the building the night before, he would have seen that the light had been bright inside the mission, but shone brighter yet on the outside as it passed through the stained glass windows. The old church had been supernaturally aglow in the darkness on the hill. The brilliantly lit windows could be seen for miles in all directions as the old man's life was celebrated.

The cashier nodded a thank you. Tom took his change, and as he did so he noticed the cashier's gold wristband. It was very similar to his except the cashier's gemstone was ruby, a solid red. Tom's was an agate, a stone of many colors. It suddenly occurred to Tom that he couldn't remember the occasion for which Sharon had gotten their wristbands. Tom was unaware that Sharon couldn't remember either.

"Odd though," he thought about the cashier having a wristband almost exactly like his and Sharon's.

A crowd of spectators had begun to gather across the street, and watched as workers stripped shingles off the roof and shoved them into a molded fiberglass chute that funneled them into a dump truck parked below. Others painstakingly removed the delicate stained glass windows from aged wooden frames and packed them into a padded moving van.

A white pickup truck entered the mission parking lot and stopped near the corner. The driver got out, then, climbed into the back of the truck. He was a tall, athletically built middle-aged man. Something about his personality seemed to draw the spectators to him. His voice was deep and clear as he began to lead them in singing.

Tom started the car and drove toward the edge of the street. He shut off the engine so they could hear the people as they sang.

The singing was very good for an impromptu choir. Their songs were a tribute to the mission and the old man. The last song was one about a light that shines from within believers as they share their witness.

For a moment it seemed that each unrehearsed choir member glowed with a bright, if not brilliant, light. A worker shoving shingles off the roof had stopped to join in the singing. Exuberantly he reached for a small cylinder attached to his belt, took it in his hand and raised it above his head. A great streak of light streamed from the cylinder and burst across the sky like a bolt of lightning.

For an instant...only for an instant Tom and Sharon witnessed the flash of light.

"Did you see that?" Sharon asked as the song ended.

"I saw something," Tom said with an unsure voice. "A flash of light of some kind, I guess. But from what? And from where?"

"I don't know, Tom. It just looked...well...sort of like that flash of light we saw in Arlin's video at the meadow. It feels like we've seen this before." An involuntary shiver quivered up and down her spine as the sensation of a vacant memory returned.

"Well, we'd better be on our way," Tom said as he started the car. The powerful engine sounded its mellow roar as they drove into the street.

The man standing in the pickup truck turned and waved to them as they drove past. Both Tom and Sharon returned the wave.

"Who was that? Do we know that man?" Tom asked.

"I don't think so. We're four hundred miles from home. We've never been here before. I can't imagine that anybody in this town would know us."

"Something does seem familiar about his face though."

Charles Levi smiled from the back of the pickup as he watched the red Thunderbird drive down the hill.

CHAPTER 19

┼══╼━╾══┼

5:50 AM LOCAL TIME AUGUST 19
OVER THE INDIAN OCEAN

"Dragonfly, Dragonfly, this is Eagle's Roost. Over..."
"Dragonfly, this is Eagle's Roost. Do you copy? Over..."
"Roger, Eagle's Roost. This is Dragonfly. You are five by five. Over..."

Eagle's Roost, code name for a very high-flying AWACS aircraft, had secret, experimental radar systems, which scanned for hundreds of miles in all directions. Eagle's Roost directed all military aircraft in its patrol zone. The AWACS and its crew were referred to as the Skyboss.

"Dragonfly, switch to scrambled channel Delta Bravo Zebra. Over."

"Roger, Eagle's Roost. Switching now. Over."

Eagle's Roost had detected a surface contact in the northwest section of the Indian Ocean near the Arabian Sea. Normally a ship could be observed leaving its port and be electronically watched as it sailed upon the open ocean. This was one surface contact that was not normal, however. This contact did not appear to leave any port. It just simply appeared from nowhere, indicating that it was a surfacing submarine. The Skyboss aboard the AWACS passed this information on to Dragonfly to confirm the true identity of the surface contact.

The Skyboss wondered to himself, "Could it be the missing Iranian submarine with bow number 504 that left its port nine days ago? Would the Iranians dare launch nuclear missiles from this sub at Israel?" If so, he knew it was a sophisticated and well-equipped boat, of the older design, a K-19 class. Its electronic equipment would be very good.

Unknown to Eagle's Roost, Dragonfly had also spotted the surface contact, 65 miles away. Normally Dragonfly hunted down submerged submarines, and hunting a sub on the surface could be even more difficult because of the radar's line-of-sight characteristics.

If the submarine had surfaced, it obviously would use its own radar to detect ships and aircraft around it. So, if Eagle's Roost and Dragonfly could see the sub, then the sub could see them.

Dragonfly's crew had a rehearsed plan to overcome that situation. As the early morning sun rose in the sky, Commander Bishop pushed forward on the yoke, turned the wheel slightly to the right and pressed firmly on the rudder pedal. Dragonfly's right wing dipped as she entered a steep forward slip. After loosing 15,000 feet in altitude in less than two minutes time, the breathtaking descent left her at an altitude 50 feet above the water. Dragonfly had turned 180 degrees and flew directly toward the submarine, then disappeared below the curvature of the earth. The submarine's line of sight radar would not see her. To further avoid being detected by the submarine, Dragonfly had switched off all her forward-looking radars. For this reason she would depend on Eagle's Roost to be her eyes to guide her to the target.

The well-trained crew knew that the reason for this low altitude approach to the submarine was multi-fold. First was to gain the element of surprise by climbing up over the horizon very rapidly. Second was being able to get a visual and photographic identification before the sub could dive. The third benefit of the low altitude approach was to be able to place electronic listening devices close to the sub so as to read her electronics. The P-3 Orions, such as Dragonfly, were very good at this precise work. The missile-carrying subs that the Iranians had bought from the Soviets were lethal and sophisticated weapons, but they were not nearly as skilled at hiding as the Orions were at hunting them down.

Eagle's Roost notified Dragonfly that she was 40 miles from the sub. She continued to maintain an altitude of 50 feet. This made for dangerous flying but was very effective in being able to approach the target unseen. Commander Bishop was expert at hazardous flying. He had a steady hand and nerves of steel. He held Dragonfly straight and level as she skimmed close to the waves just 50 feet below. The early morning sunlight was bright. The sky was clear. If looking at Dragonfly from above, her white fuselage would stand out in stark contrast to the deep blue color of the water below. Cutting through the air above the waves, Dragonfly had truly assumed the characteristics of the living thing that was her namesake. She was skimming the surface of the water, searching for prey.

Commander Bishop opened the throttle to 85 percent capacity. Dragonfly's speed accelerated. This increase in speed would cut down or eliminate the sub crew's reaction time.

At a distance of 12 miles from the sub, the Tactical Officer's console sounded an alarm, indicating that the sub's radar had picked them up. Commander Bishop pulled back on the yoke to gain altitude. There was no longer any reason to try to hide. Dragonfly had successfully completed her low altitude flight. Brilliant sunlight reflected off the water. The irregular sparkling refractions struck the Dragonfly insignia painted on her fuselage making it appear alive. The gray cup gracing the maroon shield proudly proclaimed the Order of the Holy Grail. Commander Bishop slowly brought the nose up. The climbing process had to be cautious and even-handed. Climbing too quickly or too steeply could cause the tail of the aircraft to hit the water at this low altitude. By the same token, too rapid a turn to the left or the right could cause a wing tip to hit the water. Any of those situations could be fatal to Dragonfly's thirteen-man crew. Dragonfly climbed to 1,000 feet, leveled off, and slowed to 200 miles per hour.

"They're getting good at this 'cat and mouse' business," the Tactical Officer said as he reached for his intercom switch. "They're on to us now, men. Light up the forward-looking and stand by on counter measures."

First Officer Carl Jones could remember times when they could get within eight miles of a target before being painted by radar.

"Aye, aye, sir!" replied the counter measures technician. "There is no indicated threat at this time, sir."

"Stand by to launch buoys. Are you ready, Mr. Franklin?" Lt. Commander Evans asked.

"Aye, aye, sir," came the quick reply. Franklin grinned. Evans knew he was ready to launch. Asking was just a formality.

The launch of the three buoys was computer controlled. The computer calculated distance to target, speed of the aircraft, and altitude. The first buoy would be launched short and fall near the stern. The second would be launched medium range and hit the water near mid-ship. The third would be launched and strike the water beyond the bow. Franklin had already engaged the computers automatic controls.

"Good, Mr. Franklin. All hands, fifteen seconds on my mark. Four, three, two, one, mark."

Crewmen at the various stations reported to the Tactical Officer as they approached the target.

"Cameras running, sir."

"Video running, sir."

"Electronic counter measures at the ready, sir."

"Buoys away, sir!" announced Mr. Franklin as they approached the submarine.

At 1,000 feet above the water and four hundred feet to the port side of the submarine, Dragonfly sliced through the air as the buoys splashed into the water behind. Upon impact with the water, the buoys released their hydrophones and extended their antennae.

"Buoy telemetry is running, sir," Franklin reported.

"...Oh, no...no...no..." Alarm strained First Officers Jones' voice as the men listened to the intercom.

"What's wrong?" Commander Bishop demanded.

Jones was ashen faced.

"It was mighty quick, sir, but I think her missile launch doors were open!"

"Are you sure?" came a disbelieving reply.

"I've never seen that before except during a drill," Jones responded, "but I'm sure those doors were open!"

Suddenly, troubled voices on the intercom were making the

same announcement. "Her doors are open! Her doors are open!" The voices announced in heightened alarm.

The most sobering voice of all was that of Mr. Franklin. "Buoy telemetry says that her launch radars are running, sir. Launch is imminent!"

"Check that information again, Mr. Franklin," Jones replied.

"I already have, sir."

"Check again!"

"Aye, sir."

After a short pause, Franklin's nervous voice quivered as he replied in a slow and deliberate tone. "She's gonna launch for sure, sir! Her countdown is less than fifteen minutes away."

Dragonfly climbed to 5,000 feet, turned 180 degrees to reapproach the sub from the bow.

"Video confirms. She is the 504, sir."

"Thank you," Jones replied. "Keep the cameras running and pointed at that sub."

"Aye, sir," came the reply.

At a distance of one mile off the starboard side, a more detailed view of the 504 could be observed.

The crew detected no hostile intent toward them from the 504, and there were no other aircraft for two hundred miles, but as they passed by the 504 again, the terrible truth was verified. The launch doors were open. The 504 was in the launch position. This was confirmed by both visual and electronic means.

"Eagle's Roost, this is Dragonfly. Over."

"Go ahead, Dragonfly. Over."

"We can confirm. This is the Iranian 504. We can also confirm that Iran is making good on its threat to destroy Israel. Her launch doors are open. We anticipate launch in ten minutes. Repeat. She will launch! We can confirm! Over."

"Transmit all visual and electronic telemetry to us now! Over."

"Roger, Eagle's Roost. We are transmitting to you immediately and to Mideast Command at Cheyenne Mountain. Are there any other armed aircraft in our area that can get to this target before those missiles are launched? Over."

"...I regret to say, Dragonfly, the closest armed aircraft are nearly 300 miles away. They would need to be at the target in one or two minutes. That, sir, is impossible. Over."

"…I understand Eagle's Roost. Over."

Commander Bishop thought, "If only Dragonfly had just one harpoon missile…just one…we could stop this launch!" He gripped the yoke wheel tightly in frustration.

Dragonfly had flown past the 504 and was approximately six miles off the stern. She made a 180 degree turn to make yet another pass at the 504.

Again, Franklin's voice pierced the intercom. This time a hint of apprehension tainted the sound of his words. His ever-present smile was missing. "She'll launch in less than two minutes, sir. I'll stake my life on it."

After a silence that seemed to take hours, Dragonfly's commander responded with, "Mr. Franklin, we all just staked our lives on it. We must stop that launch!"

All the crewmen heard Bishop's voice. Each man clearly realized his destiny. The hours they had spent together in closed meetings…searching…searching…with questions, were at this pivotal moment rewarded with answers. To the crewmen of other aircraft they seemed odd and set apart. What the other crews could not have known was that Dragonfly's crew had been chosen and sanctified for a higher purpose.

The crew of Dragonfly was prepared to stop the mass murder of an entire unsuspecting nation. By giving up their lives, this leader and twelve men were about to stamp their fingerprints on human history.

Launch time was down to ninety seconds. The decision had been made. There was only one choice.

"…Include all intercom communication in telemetry broadcast," ordered Commander Bishop. "The whole world should know what is happening here today."

Switches were thrown.

Eagle's Roost and others were listening.

After a short pause, and with a swallow of resolve, the commander uttered the most powerful words he had ever spoken. "Men of Dragonfly, today we have the opportunity to excel. We are about to drink from the Grail of ultimate sacrifice. Gentlemen, prepare to taste the bitter wine of sweet victory!"

Commander Bishop's knuckles turned white as he gripped the four throttles and determinedly pushed them forward. The First Officer's left hand rested atop the Commander's as they opened the throttles to 110 percent. Together they pushed on their steering yokes.

The intercom went silent.

Dragonfly nosed over into a dive and was aimed directly at the base of the 504's conning tower. She groaned, creaked, and shuddered under the strain of engines screaming at full power, like the roar of a warrior rushing into battle with his sword at the ready. It seemed that even Dragonfly knew that her intended and final purpose was straight ahead.

The split second timing and catastrophic events seemed to be orchestrated by a mighty hand. Just as Dragonfly's nose passed over the stern launch tube, a missile leaped from the bowels of the 504. The missile nose cone struck Dragonfly in the belly between her wings. The warhead was designed to detonate after sub-orbital reentry at a preset altitude. It wasn't supposed to detonate so soon after launch. But it did, along with the other nine warheads the 504 was carrying.

Dragonfly and the 504 simply ceased to exist. They became as one in the mist of billions of gallons of vaporized seawater. From twenty-three thousand five hundred miles in space, the unblinking eye of a satellite camera was witness to the largest manmade explosion ever detonated in the history of the earth. It first recorded the brilliant flash. Then, it captured the donut ring of compressed air from the massive shock wave as it rushed across the ocean's surface and away from the epicenter of the blast. The white ring grew larger and larger as it raced hundreds of miles per hour across the water.

The camera recorded the giant mushroom cloud and the fireball within. It marked the spot on earth where enemies were vanquished and heroes were made.

The mushroom cloud that rose sixty thousand feet into the air cast a long, dark, and ominous shadow of destruction across sunlit water.

Forces of evil had attempted to thrust their power into the world to accomplish their desires through men. Other men had been supernaturally empowered to stop them. Again Lord of all creation had overcome the master of evil.

"Dragonfly, Dragonfly, this is Eagle's Roost. Over..."

"Dragonfly, Dragonfly, this is Eagle's Roost. Do you copy? Over."

With a note of desperation..."Dragonfly...Dragonfly...this is Eagle's Roost. Come in please. Over."

"Dragonfly...this is Eag..."

CHAPTER 20

T om and Sharon drove past the artfully carved wooden sign welcoming visitors into the Great Smoky Mountains National Park. They looked forward with great anticipation to their week-long second honeymoon in such a picturesque place. They passed through the birch forest near the ranger station at Sugarland and began the long climb up the scenic mountain. Further up the mountain, some brave climbers sat high atop the Chimney Rock and watched the red car threading its way through the trees on the road far below. From their elevated perch the hikers compared the cars to a trail of mechanical ants going up and down the mountain. Tom and Sharon absorbed the lush beauty of the forest as it showed off its late summer coat of green that showed just a hint of autumn colors to come. They watched intently for the possible sighting of a curious brown bear that might be visiting a trashcan at the roadside.

The radio station they were listening to began to fade out. Sharon turned the dial to find another station. "Must be the top of the hour. All that's on is news."

...“The best information we have from Israel at this time is that...”

Sharon turned the radio off. "Enough Mideast news!" she said. "Those people fight about something all the time. I don't want to hear the latest!"

A car approaching them from the opposite direction had not turned off the radio. The occupants of that car heard the announcer as he went on to say,

> *"Chinese involvement in the attempted attack on
> Israel is an effort to divert attention from their
> massive troop buildup on the eastern China coast.
> The Chinese were behind Iran's failed attack on
> Israel. China supplied Iran with missiles for the
> submarine and the technology to launch them. They
> wanted the Iranians to draw world attention to the
> potential nuclear destruction of Israel. They found
> willing accomplices in the Iranians. A single
> American aircraft, the Dragonfly caused that plan to
> backfire. In effect, the results desired by the Chinese
> were as planned. World attention was drawn to the
> Mideast. While the whole world was looking there,
> China used the diversion to move military hardware
> unobserved. Governments around the world and the
> UN are vehemently protesting China's involvement
> in the submarine incident and China's threats
> against Taiwan. The United States promises military
> action to honor its protection agreement with
> Taiwan should hostilities arise. This network
> learned only minutes ago that China threatened the
> United States with nuclear attack on American cities
> if there were any American involvement in opposi-
> tion to their activities. Stay tuned to this station. We
> will report details of these unprecedented events as
> they become available."*

At the crest of the mountain, at a place called Clingman's
Dome, Tom parked the car. Because Sharon had turned the radio off
they were unaware of the latest serious news. He and Sharon
walked the smooth paved trail out to the observation platform and
marveled at the beauty of the mountains. From the scenic overlook,
the highest in the park, Tom and Sharon watched the sun sink lower
in the western sky. The changing hues of reds and pinks were in
sharp contrast to the green mountains with their hazy gray tint.
Suddenly something caught their attention. A strong gust of wind
caught the top branches of the trees. The rippling of the leaves

appeared to Tom like water being churned by the wake of a boat. He felt as if it were more than just the wind that caused the movement of the leaves. Sharon shuddered as she sensed a touch of deja vu.

Tom and Sharon were the last two visitors to leave the observation point. They made their way back to their car in the remaining twilight, oblivious to others in the parking lot gathered around their cars, listening to the shocking news on the radio.

The Thunderbird's taillights disappeared into the trees as it wound its way down the highway to the valley below.

CHAPTER 21

11:16 PM LOCAL TIME AUGUST 22
NEGEV DESERT, ISRAEL

During ancient times when the Promised Land was threatened, a warrior in battle dress would climb to a high place to sound an alarm. From atop a building or a mountain, with a spear at his side, he blew through the ram's horn, the shofar. As he blew into the shofar a sound was created that carried for miles, warning of danger. Three thousand years later, in the same land, another sound echoed that warning.

Air raid sirens wailed throughout Israel. The Israeli military was on unprecedented high alert. Israeli citizens were aware that their nation had come dangerously close to being incinerated by a nuclear strike. They knew who was responsible. Retaliation in kind against Iran had just been initiated, an attack of sudden, fierce revenge. A punishing deathblow would be dealt to the capital city of the nation that would attempt to annihilate Israel.

Since the days of the Iran/Iraq war, Iran had not engaged in any major military conflicts. As a result, its military capability was strong and had not been depleted over the years. The missile defense systems around Teheran had been upgraded with the latest technology, supplied to the Iranians by the Chinese.

In response to this information, the Israeli military and the intelligence-gathering Massad developed a secret course of action. The need to overpower the complicated defense system around Teheran necessitated the activation of a specially trained squadron of F-15 fighter-bombers as the retaliatory strike force. Operation Swift Sword was born.

The Israelis knew it would be impossible for their aircraft and helicopters to avoid detection. American satellites and AWACS aircraft could record their every move. They knew the Americans would protest their actions in an effort to prevent a nuclear war from spreading. The Americans would try to persuade their Israeli ally to call back the retaliatory strike. By the time they determined that the Israelis would not be stopped it would be too late to notify Iran to defend itself. The Israeli retaliation scheme was designed with diplomatic lying and government foot dragging in mind to buy time for the F-15s to do their job.

As the sirens blared, five F-15 fighter-bomber pilots meticulously performed last minute pre-flight inspections of their aircraft. Each F-15 was carrying two air-to-air missiles and one nuclear bomb; the rest of the payload consisted of jet fuel. The planes were routinely painted a desert camouflage. But, as an act of defiance, the Israeli Air Force had authorized painting the vertical stabilizers, the tail sections of each aircraft white. On the white background was an impressive blue Star of David. The stated intention of painting this insignia was to let the world know with certainty what delivered the mighty blow...the elite Joshua Squadron.

Piloting these aircraft were five of the most proficient and highly trained men in the Israeli Air Force. Precision flying was a necessary element of one secret operation to deceive the Iranians. The operation had been designed years earlier. It had been rehearsed many times. The Israelis knew that eventually Operation Swift Sword would be used. They just didn't know when or against whom, until two days earlier when a single American aircraft named Dragonfly and her crew of 13 men gave their lives to save the nation of Israel.

Darkness had fallen and floodlights bathed the ramp when the F-15s taxied away from their secured hangar. The ground crews saluted as the planes rolled past. The pilots returned the salutes and each gave a high thumbs up. The aircraft taxied out of the floodlit area and into the partial darkness at the end of the runway. At the leader's command the planes began their take-off rolls. As speed increased, afterburners ignited. With an explosive roar their afterburners vibrated the desert floor. The release of power was so intense that observers a half mile away could feel their clothing tremble on their bodies. The aircraft with their load of nuclear weapons took off in a five-unit formation. The blue flames of the Joshua Squadron disappeared into the night.

Three hours earlier, just at dusk, a detachment of helicopters left an Israeli airbase. The objective was to fly the helicopters out of Israel, across Jordan, and into the Saudi Arabian desert. They were to intentionally violate Jordanian and Saudi Arabian airspace. By flying low over valleys, and through canyons and mountain passes, they avoided areas routinely swept by enemy radar. The helicopters were to travel to an abandoned airstrip in Saudi Arabia's northeast desert. The airstrip had been built by the Americans during the First Persian Gulf War. It was left there as a pre-positioned asset in case it should be needed again. The Israelis needed it. They chose not to ask permission to use it.

Cargo helicopters loaded with jet fuel, and Blackhawks carrying commandos, were escorted by a squadron of well-armed Apache helicopters as they moved toward a rendezvous with the F-15s. To complete their mission the F-15s required refueling. The refueling operation could not be done by tanker in the air because of enemy radar detection, thus the need for a ground-refueling stop. Israeli commandos aboard the troop carriers would secure the area around the landing strip. Helicopter gun ships would fly aerial support. Then cargo helicopters converted to tankers would refuel the F-15s when they landed at the once-abandoned desert airstrip.

The timeless conditions of the desert had molded a way of life for a group of nomadic people, known as Bedouins, who grazed sheep and goats in meager pastures, scarce of grass or vegetation. This particular star-filled night one of the nomadic families was carrying out the mundane activities they routinely performed at the end of each day. The herdsmen and their families bathed in the shallow stream, cooked their evening meal, and prepared to rest for the night in the tents they carried with them as they traveled about the desert.

When darkness came the air cooled quickly. Animals settled in for the night and huddled together to preserve warmth. Scorching days and frigid nights were expected in the Saudi Arabian desert.

The soft clink of cookware, along with muffled voices, could be heard around several fires. The smell of cooked food still lingered in the air. The chief herdsman's favorite dog crept ever closer to his master and to the radiance of the small fire, savoring its warmth. As the night air cooled, the dog inched closer to the warmth of the fire. With a grin, his master watched. It happened every night, just another simple piece of entertainment that momentarily warmed the human heart. The favorite dog had special privileges. Since part of his unofficial job was to bring comfort and friendship to his master, he had earned the privilege of closeness. The other dogs were trained specifically to protect the herd. Soon after being fed those dogs took up their positions around the camp perimeter. Curled up near scrub bushes or rocks for warmth, they waited out the night while they rested.

The small herd had its own customary practices as well. The goats and sheep huddled together after being rounded up by the dogs. An occasional bleat or baaaa could be heard as they settled down for the night. The camels, however, grunted, snorted and groaned as if they were in pain. They wallowed, scooted and squirmed to a more comfortable resting place. The night sounds became softer as the time wore on. When sleep came, all was quiet except for deep breathing and the occasional loud snore that came from one of the tents.

Suddenly, as if choreographed and well rehearsed, the animals' heads sprang up. Ears were at attention. The dogs on the herd perimeter were first on their feet. The herd animals jumped in unison to their feet. They remained at attention, listening and look-ing nervously into the dark of night.

The shuffle awoke the herdsmen. They too sat up listening. Years of experience told them that the animals sensed a threat that spooked the entire camp. The herdsmen cautiously arose from their mats and opened their tent flaps to look out. The perimeter dogs were not sounding any alarm, but were keenly watchful and on guard. Two camels went through contortions to get to their feet, while the others fidgeted anxiously, as if to say that they were not going to get up unless it was really worth their effort.

Three minutes of being pushed to the edge of panic seemed to be a very long time. The herdsmen didn't understand the cause. Fear had the herd captured in its grip. Their legs and bodies now trembled from the tension.

The peaceful Saudi Arabian night was shaken to its foundations by a loud beating, pulsating noise that seemed to shake the startled soul. That sound accompanied by the high-pitched whine of turbine-powered helicopters under heavy load and running at full power, was enough to terrify any unsuspecting man or beast. Three groups of helicopters passed over the herd at low altitude and at high speed. They were running without lights. No one ever got a good look at the monsters in the night.

The spooked animals behaved as tropical aquarium fish darting in uniform panic. The reclining camels wasted no time scrambling to their feet and breaking into a galloping run. The herdsmen yelled curses at the suddenly empty sky. Dust and animal bleats and snorts filled the air. The dogs rounded up the herd, nudging the animals back to the safety of the camp.

In two hours most of the herd was back in camp, with only stragglers yet to be rounded up. Nervousness still filled the air but calm seemed to be slowly moving in. Some of the herdsmen walked among the animals to reassure them. Two others rekindled a fire for cooking, since it appeared that some of them would be awake the rest of the night.

With absolutely no warning, the night was split again by a heart-seizing roar. Five F-15s followed the path of the helicopters, which had passed over earlier. Their speed allowed no advance warning. The second explosion of sound was mightier than the first.

A panicked stampede ensued. Tents were knocked flat. Terrified animals ran in all directions, fueled by fear unto death. Even the dogs dove for cover. Camels trampled the downed tents. Two herdsmen picked up rifles and fired bullets at the five F-15s that by then were far distant. In the panic one frustrated herdsman grabbed a piece of firewood, angrily throwing it at the departing jets. The firewood tumbled end over end, making flaming orange spirals as it completed its defiant arc through the air. The impotent weapon landed directly on top of his collapsed tent and set it afire. Barking dogs, bleating sheep and goats, and angry curses filled the once peaceful night.

The helicopter contingent of Operation Swift Sword approached the abandoned airstrip. The troop carriers landed and some of the Israeli commandos took up defensive positions, while others placed laser runway markers to guide the F-15s. Four helicopter gunships orbited the airstrip area, searching for any sign of danger. The helicopters carrying fuel tanks were put in position and their crews prepared to refuel the F-15s. Maneuvers· had been precisely executed. The Joshua Squadron landed right on cue.

The successful arrival at the desert airstrip was only part of the total scenario. It was a staging point for an elaborately planned strike against Teheran. The Israeli military and the Massad had woven a delicate web of deceit.

El Arabian Airways Flight 1099 originated in Tripoli, Libya, and flew to Alexandria, Egypt, then to Musqat, Oman with final destination Teheran, Iran. It was noted for its adherence to precisely scheduled flight times. El Arabian boasted its punctuality at every opportunity. That is precisely why the Massad selected Flight 1099 for the plan.

A Massad agent was placed in each terminal visited by Flight 1099. Since the international air traffic control language was English, the Massad agents had no difficulty discerning information concerning their targeted aircraft. The agents used scrambled radio transmissions to report pertinent details concerning 1099 to their Massad headquarters in Tel Aviv. The information in turn was relayed to the appropriate military authority.

At Tripoli and Alexandria, the progress of Flight 1099 was systematically monitored and thoroughly reported by Massad agents. At Oman the circumstances for Flight 1099 were dramatically different.

Outside the perimeter fence at the Oman airport, and within sight of the taxiway, an Israeli commando marksman and his assistant took up camouflaged positions. They lay in wait for Flight 1099. The marksman was armed with, among other weapons, a 50-caliber single shot long barrel rifle with a powerful starlight scope, zeroed at 1,000 yards. A scrambled radio message from the Massad agent inside the terminal to the waiting marksman identified Flight 1099's tail number, which would be easily seen through the starlight scope.

At 12:42 a.m., the 737 airliner Flight 1099 passed 1,000 yards in front of the expert marksman. No breeze stirred. The marksman placed the crosshairs directly on the nose gear wheels. The camouflaged enclosure muffled the powerful report from the fifty caliber round. The single bullet pierced and blew out one of the two tires. The 737 shuddered to a stop as the tire went flat. El Arabian Airline's reputation for strict, on-time service was seriously jeopardized. It was not immediately apparent that a bullet caused the blown out tire. It was viewed by the airport mechanics as just a flat tire. There was no cause for alarm, but a two-hour delay was inevitable, either to transfer passengers to another aircraft or change the wheel. Because they did not want to officially admit that there was a flaw in their otherwise unblemished schedule, Teheran was not notified that Flight 1099 was delayed.

That failure to relay information was an anticipated blessing. When the Massed agent reported this bit of news, the Israelis determined that manna from heaven comes in many forms.

The timing for the disabling of Flight 1099 was very nearly perfect. The refueled F-15s sat on the secluded desert airstrip with engines running. When the coded message, "Goliath is down" came from Oman, the F-15s were ordered to proceed with the mission.

Once again Israeli F-15s pierced the night sky as they roared away from the primitive airstrip. Just as before, they continued their clandestine flight through darkened skies, maneuvering low over desert valleys, threading and banking their way single-file through perilous mountain passes.

These expertly executed maneuvers protected the F-15s from enemy radar. They relentlessly followed their planned route across the northeast Saudi Arabian desert. On they flew until they reached a point that intersected with the normal flight path of El Arabian Flight 1099. The timing was perfect. At the intersection of routes, the attacking aircraft assumed a dramatically different attitude in flying. No longer were they twisting, turning, and banking in single file as they hugged low to the ground. In concert, the five aircraft united in an extraordinarily tight formation. With wingtip to wingtip and nose to tail, distances between the aircraft were measured in inches. They became as one flying unit.

Four pilots followed their leader intently, mirroring his every move as he turned north toward Teheran. With singleness of purpose the unit gradually rose to an altitude of twenty-nine thousand feet, assuming the course and speed that the disabled airliner would have taken had it continued its journey. At that point the tightly grouped Joshua Squadron **became** the delayed El Arabian Airways Flight 1099.

Only the lead pilot operated an identification transponder. The other four switched theirs off. Instead of transmitting the code identifying the aircraft as F-15s, the one transponder code identified all five aircraft as a single Boeing 737. When the inbound air traffic controller at Teheran viewed a blip on his radar screen, showing air speed, altitude, estimated arrival time, airline, flight, and tail number, he mentally noted that Flight 1099 was, as always, right on time.

Maintaining the descent angle the airliner would have taken, the F-15s descended in altitude as they approached the Teheran airport. The deception continued as the lead pilot communicated to the air traffic controller the intent to land.

The deception ended fifty miles out when each plane abruptly broke formation and rushed at high speed to its individual target in the Teheran area. At twenty miles from their separate targets each F-15 released its "launch and forget" satellite guided nuclear bomb. Immediately upon bomb release, the attacking aircraft banked and turned sharply toward their home base in Israel. The bombs continued their flight toward their pre-programmed targets, giving time for the Joshua Squadron to engage their afterburners and escape from the blast that was sure to come.

As the Teheran air traffic controller managed other aircraft in his sector he was startled to observe 1099 suddenly transform from a single aircraft into 5 separate blips. In confusion he observed the images on his radarscope. The controller keyed his microphone to question the captain of Flight 1099. The response from the lead F-15 pilot was the two thousand year old phrase, "NEXT YEAR IN

JERUSALEM!!!"

The controller watched in horror, as the five blips became ten blips. Bombs had been released.

Operation Swift Sword was exacting Israel's revenge.

"No, No, No!" he shouted into the microphone as he sprang suddenly to his feet, tipping his chair and sending it crashing to the floor.

One last agonizing shout of "Noooo!!!" was silenced by the searing white-hot burst of a thermo nuclear explosion.

CHAPTER 22

Ignoring the news was no longer possible. Teheran was the topic of conversation every place Tom and Sharon went in the Smoky Mountains. They discovered that a switched off radio would not prevent bad news from being reported, only delay their hearing about it. They experienced an urgent need to surround themselves with the familiarity of home.

Sunrise found the T-bird creeping along in heavy northbound interstate traffic. News of world events had blanketed the nation. It seemed that everyone had a sense of urgency to be someplace else. The interstate highway was choked with travelers. Because of the congestion it was rumored that the interstate highway system would be closed to all but military traffic, allowing easy access to military convoys. Tom decided to leave the interstate and travel the secondary roads. Instead of enjoying a beautiful, relaxing, scenic drive, bodies were tensed as their attention was focused on the road-way and the radio news.

... *"Because of the Teheran bombing, Arab insurgents have attacked Israel along all the Jordanian borders. These attacks seem to be carried out in small clusters of terrorists rather than an invasion by armies from neighboring nations. Conjecture from high-ranking military consultants in Washington seems to be that the nations want to avoid nuclear confrontation. The United States is urging all parties to cease-fire and come to a peaceful resolution of the crisis before the situation becomes an all-out war, officials reported..."*

The station faded away; another was quickly found. The news was all the same. War seemed all too likely.

Once Tom and Sharon crossed the Ohio River, the landscape changed from Kentucky mountains to the flatter rolling hills of southern Indiana. Soon familiar roads and scenery offered needed comfort. Just at dusk the T-bird rolled down Highway 93. As they drove past the meadow, the radio blared a special bulletin.

..."The Pentagon has just announced that China has invaded Taiwan and, in a joint effort, North Korean and Chinese troops have invaded South Korea. The United States is sending naval battle groups into the area in an effort to protect U.S. interests there. The Japanese Home Defense Guard is on full alert. Stay tuned to this station. We will update you as reports of this breaking news come in to us."

Throughout the evening Tom and Sharon, as well as people all over the nation, gathered in their homes to listen to radio and television news.

As was his usual routine, Steve Nicholson surveyed his surroundings before retiring for the night. Tonight it was past his normal bedtime as he stepped out onto his back porch. The air seemed unusually cool on this late summer evening, possibly ushering in an early fall. A brisk breeze blew the chilly air through the fibers of his shirt.

A muffled, metallic tapping sound from somewhere in the darkness caught his attention. He stepped cautiously from the porch onto the grass and into the total darkness of his familiar backyard. As his eyes slowly became accustomed to the lack of light, he could faintly see a loose section of antenna cable flapping like a flag against his metal radio tower. Steve reasoned that the thunderstorm earlier in the day had blown the cable loose. He made a mental note to repair the cable the next morning.

As his eyes became fully adjusted to the darkness, he scanned the tower from the pedestal at the bottom to the antenna at the top. Steve looked past the antenna and out to the stars. Their brilliance took his breath away. The Milky Way was a great luminous streak curving through the night sky. The earlier storm had washed the air so clean that it allowed the usually hidden natural beauty to be displayed with revealing clarity. He soaked in the majesty above.

As Steve turned to go back into the house, his gaze scanned the wooded area to his left and the open fields in front of him. He paused for a moment to consider a distant glow on the horizon that he had not noticed before. Somewhat dim at first, the glow became brighter. The bright lights of a far away outdoor sports stadium came to his mind.

The once cool breeze turned penetratingly cold. Steve shivered as he returned to the porch. As he reached for the handle on the glass door an unusual reflection caught his eyes. He turned suddenly to see that the glow had become a very bright pinpoint of light just above the horizon.

Steve observed the light, glowing ever brighter with each passing second. He nervously swallowed hard and hurried into the house. He quickly located the binoculars and returned to the porch, knocking a rocking chair awry. Adrenaline pumped throughout his body. His heart raced wildly. His skin became clammy as a quick glance through the binoculars confirmed what he feared.

At an altitude of five thousand feet the nuclear fiend had been released. The sub orbital missile had found its target. Ground zero was a point near Chicago's Lakeshore Drive.

Almost instantly the temperature within a one-mile radius of the center of the explosion flared to the temperature of the sun. Heat and light flashed from the epicenter of the explosion at incredible speed. Combustible materials exploded into flame as a firestorm instantly spread. Stone, steel and bricks melted. Less substantial material simply evaporated. Cars in the street vaporized. Buildings and trees ignited like matches.

Temperatures decreased as the distance from the center of the blast increased. The firestorm began to lessen at about ten miles.

Behind the firestorm came the devastating donut ring, a shock wave that rushed outward in all directions from the center of the blast. Burning buildings exploded and flaming trees were ripped from the ground. The destructive ability of the shock wave diminished as its distance from the center of the blast increased. Twenty miles from the center, the shock wave had slowed at its far reaches and weakened to a standstill.

A new phenomenon developed. The air currents reversed directions back toward ground zero. The nuclear fireball and intense heat had created a tremendous vacuum that caused the winds to rush over the surface of the ground at ever-increasing speeds to fill the void. The hurricane force wind picked up millions of pieces of debris. It threw them violently into the fireball that rose above what had been the city. Dust, dirt and burning material, as well as steam from partially vaporized Lake Michigan, rose to form a great mushroom cloud illuminated from within by the rising fireball.

In less than one minute most of Chicago was destroyed. The boiling, churning cloud rose to an altitude of sixty thousand feet and was clearly seen from as far away as the Nicholsons' home in Indianapolis. Steve's eyes widened as his heartbeat pounded in his ears.

"It's really happening!" Steve cried out as he raced back into the house.

"Get up!" he demanded loudly to his sleeping wife and son. "Get UP! Get on your feet! Get up NOW! Don't think! Just DO what I tell you! Grab warm clothes, coats, pillows, and blankets," he ordered Linda and Andy.

Steve's urgency pierced their sleepy minds and they responded automatically to his urgency. They took their possessions to the already well-provisioned basement shelter.

Steve grabbed the telephone. "Tom!" Steve shouted into the phone. "Get up now! Somebody just nuked Chicago!"

Steve penetrated Tom's drowsy mind by repeating, "Somebody nuked Chicago! Grab your stuff and get over here now! I'll call Arlin and Maggie. You call Jim."

Tom's call to Jim Newland prompted Jim to go to a prepared shelter closer to his home.

Tom and Sharon rushed from their house. The distant trees blocked their view of the horizon. From their house upon the hill, the Browns, however, had a good view of the brilliantly illuminated mushroom cloud one hundred seventy miles to the north.

The Browns arrived in their car at the same time as the Alexanders, who arrived on foot and out-of-breath. They entered the Nicholson home together for what they knew would be a long stay.

Linda grabbed the clipboard that hung by a rawhide string from a nail beside the basement entrance. She called out orders and made assignments from a prepared checklist. The Nicholson shelter burst alive with activity. Tom started the air filter system. Arlin and Maggie topped off the water tanks, and then turned off the outside water source. Andy and Sharon nailed shut the outside windows as well as the door leading inside the house and sealed them all with caulk and plastic sheets. Steve tested the diesel generator's remote starter. When he pushed the button the generator immediately rattled to life. As he shut it off, Steve breathed a sigh of relief, knowing that if the power failed they would have the generator for electricity. They all examined the shelter carefully to discover any crack or opening that could be a source for contaminated dust to enter the living area. The written checklist was inspected for the final time. All items were checked off. The outside door was sealed and nailed shut.

Steve switched on his radio. Reception was poor and getting worse every minute. Electromagnetic pulses caused by nuclear detonation interfered with reception but he was still able to learn that Chicago was not the only American city hit. Radio reception soon disappeared. He could only wonder when the radio could be used again.

The seven people in Steve's well-organized basement shelter knew enough about a nuclear explosion to know that there were not words strong enough to describe the horror.

The hunkering down had begun.

CHAPTER 23

⊢⟩═══⟨⊣

Static hissed and sizzled as Steve tuned the radio while Tom adjusted the antenna rotor. Their unceasing attempts to locate a national radio station were in vain. Frustration grew as those who had gathered in Steve's basement realized they no longer had contact with the outside world. National communications systems had been virtually destroyed. Internet and telephone connections were dead. For a short period of time the only means of electronic communication was the limited amount that could be received by local radio. Many radio and television stations had suddenly disappeared from the airwaves due to nuclear interference. Severe damage to the national electrical power grid caused some stations to leave the air. All other stations were ordered off the air by the FCC to prevent other missiles from using radio and TV signals as homing beacons to locate American cities. Emergency planners anticipated more missiles. Yet none came. After three days the FCC relaxed the restrictions and allowed selected local stations to broadcast at very low power in order to provide citizens with local information.

For the next two months the atmosphere was exasperating for the seven people in the basement shelter. They had received very limited communication with the outside world. From their own eyewitness experience they knew the United States had been hit with nuclear weapons but they didn't know why they were attacked nor by whom. The extent of the damage was unknown to them. Speculation of possible future events caused the seven to live with many moments of anxiety. The local low power emergency station provided little help with news of world events. Its broadcasts consisted mainly of official instructions for the local Indianapolis area. Steve surmised that either there was no news from the outside world or the station was somehow prohibited from broadcasting it. This simply added to the frustration they already felt. Conditions in the shelter were smothering. Although all parties were long-time and treasured friends none were accustomed to such tension, which only increased as the weeks went by.

As the nation's power grid came back on line bits and pieces of news slowly began trickling in, yet not enough for them to fully understand the entire series of events. It was broadcast that the devastation was great but there were many survivors. Tensions among the seven were somewhat relieved in the basement shelter with even this small amount of news. Worse than knowing bad news was not knowing any news.

One gray, misty morning Steve unexpectedly heard an intermittent signal on the radio. He frantically adjusted the frequency. A voice often disregarded by the public yet so familiar to Steve broke through the static. The talk show host, once categorized by the majority as a political fanatic, was once again on the air nationally.

"Some of you have been able to receive this program for a few weeks now. You are aware of current world news. Many of you are receiving this program for the first time. For that reason during the first half of every hour we will recap the history of this short war. You people out there who have radios spread the word to those who don't. People need to know what's going on.

"Just as World War II had its Day of Infamy this war had its Awful Day. Since the war lasted only six hours the Awful Day was the totality of the war. No one really wanted to believe that day would come. A few were aware of the 'saber rattling' preceding it. They heard the threats and saw the troop movements. They sounded the alarm. Some listened. Most

did not. Most believed that some how, some way, some thing would prevent that Awful Day. The Most were wrong. The Awful Day came.

"During the immediate aftermath survivors studied the causes. In an unexpected event, China turned its military aggression toward Japan. The Chinese threatened to take Taiwan by force if Taiwan declared her independence. Two days after the Teheran bombing the Chinese invaded Taiwan, Japan, and South Korea. Masses of Chinese troops moved by air, land and sea in almost every type of conveyance possible. True to their pragmatic mindset, they made it happen. The loss of life was tremendous. This proved to be of little concern to the Chinese army. With 1.2 billion in their country they had many lives to use.

"The invasion of Taiwan and South Korea was somewhat expected. The total surprise was the massive invasion of Japan by the Chinese. With the loss of the Japanese islands as a base of operations, Western powers led by the United States sustained a severe loss in their military supply line. This loss of military bases and supplies caused the defenders of Japan to counterattack.

"Sea power was the key. When the Chinese used one of their cruisers purchased from the Russians to fire a nuclear missile at the massive aircraft carrier USS Ronald Reagan, the lock that contained the demons was opened. In one swift blow, a single nuclear missile sunk the Reagan with its crew of 8,000 men aboard. One eighth of American sea power in the Pacific was lost with the firing of one missile. American military commanders could not tolerate the loss.

"The United States Navy responded by launching nuclear missiles at the attacking Chinese naval vessels. The fighting escalated. From under two miles of granite in Colorado, the observers in Cheyenne Mountain watched the situation unfold and sounded the alarm. Computers plotted missile paths on the giant screen.

"Beijing launched Intercontinental Ballistic Missiles at the United States. Los Angles, San Francisco, Chicago and New York were hit. America retaliated against Chinese cities. Because the Chinese struck U.S. population centers instead of missile launching centers, little damage was done to America's ability to retaliate and defend her survivors.

"Pakistan used the Chinese missile activity as an opportunity to attack its age old foe, India, in their dispute over the province of Cashmere. The Indian government responded. The nuclear demon spread throughout parts of Asia like a cancer. The authorities in Cheyenne Mountain could only watch as destruction rained from the sky.

"The Russians, smugly trying to avoid being part of a disaster in progress, waited until they could determine who the victor might be. Moscow obviously assumed that the United States would be the victor, so they abruptly struck at Western Chinese military installations. The Russians would never want to overlook an opportunity for national expansion, even if the annexed territory would glow in the dark. It is ironic that it was the Russians who supplied the equipment that started the whole disastrous scenario. Russia supplied the infamous submarine, the 504, to Iran. They also supplied the Chinese with the nuclear cruiser that sank the aircraft carrier, USS Ronald

Reagan. It was Russian war machines that initiated the nuclear disaster.

"With their remaining few missiles the Chinese struck back at Russia and devastated much of the area around Moscow.

"As suddenly as it started, it was over. The missile exchange finished only six hours after it began."

The talk show host paused for a moment then remarked, *"You know folks, the wound that was inflicted upon the earth that day could be likened to a person who severely wounded his hand with a sharp knife. He could see the danger, could see the knife slip, and watch as the ghastly wound in the hand was made. He could look at the ugly gash and not feel the pain right away. Only after the blood began to flow and an assessment of the damage was done could the full impact be felt. So it was with that day. The wound had been made. The blood was visible but the real pain had not registered.*

"In hindsight, many of you listening out there are amazed that the steps leading to this worldwide disaster were not seen but it seems so obvious to you now in retrospect." Using the trademark of pounding his fist on the desk he reflected, *"I tried to tell you people out there that the Abrams Report was to be believed. Only some of you were listening."* He characteristically rattled the papers for emphasis then continued his report.

"The Chinese incited the Iranians to use their Russian-built submarine, the 504, to attack Israel in an effort to call the world's attention away from the invasion of Taiwan, Japan and South Korea. However

the mission of attacking Israel was subsequently discovered and thwarted by the American naval aircraft Dragonfly. Israel retaliated against the threat to her homeland by sending the Joshua Squadron to destroy Teheran. The U.S. defense of Taiwan, Japan, and South Korea led to a confrontation with China and the sinking of the aircraft carrier Ronald Reagan by a Chinese nuclear missile." Once again the talk show host paused to reflect and emphatically stated, *"You people out there should have been paying attention. All these were steps that should have foretold the impending nuclear disaster. But human nature, being true to form was blind to the very things that endanger mankind most..."*

The station faded once again and Steve tried unsuccessfully to retune the radio. They all continued their daily task of searching for news. Each time they were able to receive a radio signal, they gathered more and more details.

Worldwide communications sustained severe damage. As they were slowly re-established, the disastrous results of the Awful Day were becoming known. A more complete picture was beginning to form for the survivors in the shelter.

Taiwan, the original flashpoint of the war, was virtually uninhabitable. Much of Japan was devastated. The ancient land of China was a smoking ruin. India and Pakistan were annihilated. In America the cities of Los Angeles, San Francisco, Chicago, and New York were disasters. Even now, there were reports that smoke still rose from fires smoldering deep within the rubble of these cities. Entertainment capitals of the west coast, corporate headquarters of mid-west American food distribution centers, along with the financial hub of the east coast, were ruined. Also gone was the headquarters of the United Nations, a multi-national system whose goal was to rule the world. The rest of the nation did not suffer direct hits, but the shock of an actual war on American soil had numbed the American people. Survivors resolved that a day like the Awful Day would never happen again.

CHAPTER 24

The pain from the great wound that had been inflicted upon the earth was inestimable. It was first predicted that the death toll worldwide would be counted in the millions. As information was gathered, the real death toll from direct and indirect means would be very close to 240 million people. Those remaining were incapable of understanding the magnitude of death and destruction when reports came in of whole cities being destroyed. Eventually people became numb to reports of death. The large casualty figures seemed to be foreign numbers until friends and relatives could no longer be reached. Then came the realization that they could never be reached. Life was changed. The pain from the wound grew in intensity.

Communities throughout the world had pockets of well-provisioned people, "survivalists" they were called. For three months they waited. They waited for the nuclear winter that had always been predicted by the experts. It never came. In the fourth month the rains came, a torrent at first. Then, after a week of heavy downpours, a moderate drizzle set in, washing away the radioactive dust and cleansing the air.

Recovery slowly began. Survivors gradually adjusted to a new world. For two years after the Awful Day, great effort was made to keep the great wound to humanity from hemorrhaging...to slow the death rate from secondary reasons. There were areas of the world untouched by direct disaster. In many of these areas survivalists came forward to help the unprepared, saving many lives in recovering communities. Training areas were quickly established to teach people how to protect themselves from fall-out, radiation poisoning, starvation, and from an array of diseases, including the "behavioral disease" of looting and pillaging. People were taught how to manage without electricity and other conveniences of civilization. Third world and developing countries survived the best. They were already practiced in the art of survival. In many areas of the world it was back to basics.

World financial centers had the foresight before The Awful Day to diversify their operations into other parts of the world. The largest was located in London, England and was left practically intact. The United Nations, with similar resolve, had established a great portion of its operations in Berlin, Germany. The slogan of the New United Nations was, "With **NUN** There Will Be Peace!"

This New United Nations became a formidable and treacherous regime. Under the guise of world governing assistance, the leaders of the New United Nations lured many countries to surrender their sovereignty to this consuming political power. These countries comprised the strongest consortium. When the nations' banners were unfurled, the Russian bear, the French Gaelic rooster, and the German leopard, stood side by side with flags from many smaller European nations. The most unusual and powerful group in the New United Nations was not a nation at all but an unlikely alliance of religious groups from around the world. These disparate religions melded into the most uncommon religious coalition ever assembled. The ten-man leadership in the New United Nations came from persons who held high position in this religious coalition. In a short time these ten men took complete control of the organization.

The banners most noticeably absent from the NUN Plaza of National Standards were the Stars and Stripes, the Union Jack, and the Star of David. The people of the United States again upheld the principles upon which their country was founded. They refused to surrender the sovereignty of their constitution, which said that they were guaranteed by their Creator "certain inalienable rights". This strength of conviction fueled a new fire within the remaining people of the United States. They were shunned by the rest of the world as they moved their nation in a separate direction. America's ability to recover from the effects of The Awful Day was unprecedented.

Central and southeastern areas of the United States avoided the winds that carried the fall-out belt around the world. Those who lived there were thankful that the prevailing winds carried the fall-out away. The names Nicholson, Brown, Alexander, and Newland were known throughout the area west of Indianapolis for their resourcefulness and ability to get things done. It was said by many that they seemed to be supernaturally empowered to survive and lead others in the rebuilding.

The nine years following The Awful Day were marked with recovery success stories. A great healing occurred, but just as with any massive wound that heals...a scar remains. The Awful Day left many scars: burned out cities that could only be viewed from a distance; relatives and friends who simply vanished; highways that lead to nowhere; rusted trains that sit idle on the tracks...monuments left as tributes to mankind's inability to live in peace. With the passage of time those scars have become accepted facts of life. But there are still wars and rumors of wars.

In thousands of years of history, a secret comes bubbling to the surface of this troubled cauldron. The secret is that careful study of history can predict the future; the problem is that what we learn from history is that *no one learns from history*. Mankind simply proclaims, "Peace, peace, when there is no peace."

CHAPTER 25

The radio talk show host adjusted his overstuffed chair as he assumed his usual position at his studio desk. With three minutes until airtime he pondered the words he was about to say. He knew that the microphone in front of him had a great influencing power over his approximately seventy-five million listeners. In a high-speed mental replay he recalled highlights of the past twenty-nine years of radio broadcasting. He evaluated the steps that led him to this moment.

Softly he said to himself, "There's never been a broadcast like this one, at least not from this microphone."

The host looked around the studio surveying the maze of electronic equipment that surrounded him. The red light changed to yellow, indicating fifteen seconds to airtime. At five seconds the producer held up five fingers, counted down, then pointed to the host. At one second to go the light changed to green. The microphone was hot and the show was on the air. He looked at the prepared notes in his hands, made a mental assessment, tossed the notes aside, and began to speak from his heart.

During the first few seconds millions of die-hard faithful listeners knew that something was different - very different. There was not the usual upbeat, high-energy music. The rattling of paper near the microphone was absent. The flamboyant and braggadocios voice of a Type A extrovert talk show host to which the listeners had become accustomed was not to be heard. There was none of the usual. There was only the unusual.

"Most of you people out there have been listening to this program for many years. Over time we have discussed things from the light-hearted to the serious. Through your phone calls you have made your opinions known. Together we have dialogued. Today the program will be different. No phone calls will be accepted. I have a very serious matter to talk about. Some of you already know about it. Most do not.

"When I talked to you years ago about such things that led to the First Gulf War, some of you heeded my warnings. Most did not. Years later when I warned you of the Second Gulf War, the Terrorist War, some of you heeded the warning. Most did not. Soon after that I warned you of an event that we now call The Awful Day War. Many of you heeded the warning. Most did not.

"I am about to give you another warning. This time it is imperative that you heed my warning. It is the truth of the message itself that cries out to be believed.

"You know from listening to me that I am an analytical person. It is my passion to go to great lengths to prove and double prove any thing that I say on this show. You know that I rely heavily on the Abrams Report and the dedication of the people who work there. For the last year or so the Abrams people have been using their resources to investigate certain claims. These claims have to do with the Bible, ancient tablets and writings, historical records from around the world, and most of all prophecies yet unfulfilled.

"Seventy-three days ago an astounding event took place in my life - so astounding was the event that I began to count the days of my new life. That's how I know it was seventy- three days. Each day is so precious to me that I count them as if each were a gemstone of great wealth. The dawn of each day is a thing of great joy.

"What is this great event in my life? Seventy-three days ago I became a believer in the Lord Jesus, the Son of God. My new life had begun.

"I have been a 'Doubting Thomas' all my life. I have had to have everything proven to me. Through the Abrams Report and their facilities and all the things I mentioned earlier the physical proof was laid out in front of me. The Lord then said to me, 'Here is the proof you asked for. All you have to do now is believe.' I was compelled to believe. His Spirit came over me and settled within me. I felt my nature and my thinking change. New understanding came to me. I looked at life in a new way.

"For several days I wondered what would become of the new me. I did not hear an audible voice but the Spirit within made me know that I had been guided to this time and place for a specific purpose. Jesus told us that no man comes to the Father except by Him. He also says that no man comes to Him except the Father draw him there. I was guided to that point of choice and I chose to believe. My experience as a radio talk show host is no accident. I am to use the power of this microphone to reach around the world.

"We are at this time watching prophetic events unfold world-wide. There are wars and rumors of wars, unlikely national confederations, and natural calamities of all kinds. Events are unfolding at an ever increasing rate. The events are strong and grow in strength every day. These events resemble the progression and intensity of labor pains. With the end of the pain comes the birth of the fresh and new. And so it is with the coming of our Lord. The trials will increase with intensity and frequency until Jesus comes.

"We are not to know the date or the hour of His coming but we will know when the time is near. We are told that when the leaves come out on the fig tree we will know that summer soon will follow. When the nation of Israel was formed in 1948 the leaves on the fig tree came out. There is an event of monumental importance that will mark the beginning of the season. When the time comes, the faithful will place the cornerstone to a temple to be built upon Temple Mount in Jerusalem. In two hundred eighty days from the placing of the cornerstone the temple will be complete. The Jewish worship and sacrifice will begin again. When the cornerstone is placed into position the prophetic clock will start ticking. In approximately seven years from the placing of the cornerstone the Lord Jesus will come to cleanse the earth and to claim His own. The placing of the cornerstone will be the beginning of the season. We can only wait with great expectancy for the date and the hour.

"What does all this have to do with this radio program and you and me? Well I'll tell you. Never in my life as a radio talk show host have I ever thought of myself as a preacher. I still don't. I am called to be a messenger and a witness. My witness to you is to tell you to investigate the truths of the Bible. To pray, to repent of sin, to allow the Holy Spirit to live and work within you, then to go out and convince others. Teach others the truth of God's word."

Hour after hour and day after day the talk show host made his plea. The audience grew. His previous years of broadcasting provable truth caused many to pay attention to the new program format. He was energized by a power not his own. He ended each program with, "Time is growing short. Work while there is still daylight. Darkness is coming when no work can be done."

CHAPTER 26

The world of children remains mostly free from the worries of war and peace. But worries are relative. Simple things can pack as much punch as world peace in the emotions of a child. A youngster's world can come crashing down when he is not chosen to play in a game of sandlot football. Expectantly, a little eight-year-old boy waits. He is not chosen. Dejected, he carries his helmet by the chinstrap, dragging it beside him as his cleats crunch gravel. He walks downcast toward his waiting father.

The blonde haired boy tosses his helmet on the floor of the convertible and climbs into the seat. His father slowly backs out of the parking lot, all the while wondering what to say to help his son feel better. They pull into the street and drive away. The wind dries the boy's tears.

The father reaches over and gently touches his son's chin with his fist in a gesture of friendly banter. The boy responds with a slight smile and seems comforted. The father is happy. On they drive until they reach their destination…home. The candy apple red Thunderbird turns into the long driveway.

Sharon, with her motherly intuition, waits in the yard to welcome her husband and son. A sudden gust of wind catches the top branches of the tall trees that line their driveway. The rippling of the leaves catches her attention. Sharon watches the movement to the end of the tree line. She senses a touch of deja vu.

Joseph jumps from the car and runs into his mother's out-stretched arms.

Tom and Sharon had made their choice.
Joseph...the purpose for which they had been sealed.

EPILOGUE

✛══✛

During the months and years that followed The Awful Day, the Alexander family developed a habit of sitting together on the sofa for a while just before bedtime. The practice was begun as a means of gathering the latest information from short-wave radio broadcasts from around the world. As time passed, the evening gathering continued, but the subject matter they discussed changed gradually from world events to family matters. As Joseph grew older he became more a participant in the conversation rather than the subject of it.

On this night as the little family settled into their usual perches on the sofa, both Tom and Sharon expected Joseph to talk about the playground incident earlier when he felt rejected from not being chosen to play in a childhood game. His parents were surprised that the football game was never mentioned. Instead Joseph brought up a subject that he had told them about only once before...a dream that had awakened him in the night.

As Joseph cradled his mother's arm against his chest, he absent-mindedly fingered the gold bracelet with its multi colored stone that she always wore. He leaned his left shoulder and head against Tom's right arm and settled into a comfortable niche he made for himself.

"Hey Dad," Joseph said thoughtfully.

"Yes, son?"

"Do you remember the dream I told you about where I had a whole bunch of cousins?"

While his son was speaking, Tom was reminded of the times he and Sharon had discussed naming him Joseph. They were so thrilled when they were told they would be parents…and to have a baby so long after they had given up hope. There was hardly any discussion in the matter of the name. They seemed to know from the beginning the baby would be a boy and they should name him after the Biblical Joseph. They didn't know why. It seemed so ironic now that their Joseph would also be a dreamer.

Tom answered, "Yes, I remember that you had a hundred cousins in that dream."

"I had that the dream again, Dad, and this time I had thousands of cousins!"

"A thousand cousins this time?" Tom asked.

"No, Dad, not a thousand but a lot of thousands, maybe over a hundred thousand cousins! And we were singing a happy song."

"Wow, son, that sure is a lot of relatives!"

Tom glanced at Sharon as he moved to put his arm around Joseph to pull his son closer to him. He noticed Sharon had an unusual expression on her face.

"Where do you suppose all those cousins came from, son?" Tom asked, as Sharon looked first at Joseph then at Tom.

Joseph had a ready answer. Tom had asked the question in jest, but Joseph answered quickly and with conviction.

"The cousins came from all over the world Dad."

Tom studied his son's statements and Sharon's reaction. The pause was lengthy.

"Hey Dad."

"Yes, son?"

"I dreamed that all my cousins got together in one place."

"Where is that place?"

"I don't know exactly," Joseph said. "It's a far away place that I've never been to."

Again a pause.

"Hey Dad."

"Yes, son?"

"In this place where all us cousins met, there were people trying to hurt us…and, Dad?"

"Yes, son?"

"Last night there was more to my dream. Do you want to hear it?"

"Certainly! We want to hear all of it!"

"There was a monster in my dream last night. It was trying to get me and all my thousands of cousins."

"What kind of monster was it?" Tom asked.

"Well, it looked like a leopard but it had seven heads. Its feet looked like a bear's feet and it said awful things."

"Were you afraid of the monster, son?"

"Oh, no, Dad. The monster never wins!"

Sharon gasped at a sudden and vivid memory of a man named Charles and a message he had given them years before. A message of a choice that they would make, the promises he foretold for their then yet-to-be conceived son, and of a gathering of the tribes of Israel in Jerusalem. Sharon was at peace with the knowledge that their son would be protected from spiritual harm as she and Tom had been.

Joseph was sealed for his purpose to be a great man for God. As it was on The Awful Day, so it was later when the radio announcement was made. Some were listening. Most were not.

... "We interrupt this program to bring you a special news bulletin from the New United Nations headquarters in Berlin, Germany. The NUN Secretary General has announced a confirmation of a covenant among the Israelis, Palestinians and Arabs. The covenant permits the Palestinians to build their capitol in East Jerusalem and allows the Israelis to build a temple on Temple Mount. For many of the Jewish faith the cry will finally be realized, NEXT YEAR IN JERUSALEM! The Secretary General stated today that this much-sought-after and elusive covenant agreement is confirmed and guaranteed by the power of the New United Nations. This co-existence had been a sticking point in negations for generations. This ends an era of haggling

and table pounding by both parties. In his speech today, the politically powerful Secretary General assured the world that peace and safety is imminent in the Mideast. Member nations of the NUN are celebrating this announcement by proclaiming national holidays and declaring peace, peace, peace at last."

The Jewish Faithful presented the cornerstone to the Israeli government. Permission was granted. The temple will be built. The countdown has begun for the gathering of the tribes of Israel from the four corners of the earth.

THE BEGINNING...OF THE END.

*"And I saw another angel ascending from the east, having the seal of the living God: and he cried with a loud voice to the four angels, to whom it was given to hurt the earth and the sea, Saying, Hurt not the earth, neither the sea, nor the trees, till we have sealed the servants of our God in their foreheads. And I heard the number of them which were sealed: and there were sealed an hundred and forty and four thousand of all the tribes of the children of Israel. Of the tribe of Juda were sealed twelve thousand. Of the tribe of Reuben were sealed twelve thousand. Of the tribe of Gad were sealed twelve thousand. Of the tribe of Aser were sealed twelve thousand. Of the tribe of Nephthalim were sealed twelve thousand. Of the tribe of **Manasses** were sealed twelve thousand. Of the tribe of Simeon were sealed twelve thousand. Of the tribe of Levi were sealed twelve thousand. Of the tribe of Issachar were sealed twelve thousand. Of the tribe of Zabulon were sealed twelve thousand. Of the tribe of Joseph were sealed twelve thousand. Of the tribe of Benjamin were sealed twelve thousand."*

Rev 7:2-8 (KJV)

"And I looked, and, lo, a Lamb stood on the mount Sion, and with him an hundred forty and four thousand, having his Father's name written in their foreheads. And I heard a voice from heaven, as the voice of many waters, and as the voice of a great thunder: and I heard the voice of harpers harping with their harps: And they sung

as it were a new song before the throne, and before the four beasts, and the elders: and no man could learn that song but the hundred and forty and four thousand, which were redeemed from the earth. These are they which were not defiled with women; for they are virgins. These are they which follow the Lamb whithersoever he goeth. These were redeemed from among men, being the firstfruits unto God and to the Lamb."

Rev 14:1-4 (KJV)

"When ye therefore shall see the abomination of desolation, spoken of by Daniel the prophet, stand in the holy place, (whoso readeth, let him understand:)"

Matt 24:15 (KJV)

"So likewise ye, when ye shall see all these things, know that it is near, even at the doors."

Matt 24:33 (KJV)

NOTES

Within the text of this novel there are events that are parallel to events in the Bible. Scripture references below are listed by chapter.

Chapter One: Ezekiel 1:13, 14 * Nahum 2:4

Chapter Four: Matthew 24:1, 2

Chapter Six: 1 Samuel 13

Chapter Eight: II Kings 6:17 * 1 Kings 6 * Exodus 39 * Leviticus 23:27, 28, 25:9 Numbers 19:1, 2, 9 * Numbers 19:1, 2, 9 * Genesis 25:16-18

Chapter Nine: 2 Kings 6:17 * Psalm 89:6, 7, 9, 11, 93:1, 2, 97:1, 119:96 * 1 Corinthians 2:9, 15:41 * Psalm 19:1, 50:6, 8:1, 27, Deuteronomy 4:19 * Psalm 91:11, 19:1 * II Corinthians 12:2-3 * I Corinthians 2:9 * Romans 1:25 * Genesis 7:17-24, 8:1, 2 * Revelation 12:9 * John 8:44 * Romans 1:18-22, 1:32 * Genesis 1:1-26 * John 1:1 * 1 John 5:7, 8 (KJV) * Isaiah 30:26 * Job 22:12 * Psalm 37:4, 147:4 * Isaiah 60:20 * Revelation 21:23 * Acts 8:39

Chapter Thirteen: Job:26:14 * Ephesians 6:12-18 * Exodus 39:14 * Psalm 3:3, 18:35 * Ephesians 6:16 * 2 Thessalonians 2:3, 4 * 2 Corinthians 4:3, 4, 11:14 * Ephesians 5:1-4 * 1 Colossians 16:13 * Galatians 5:1 * Philippians 1:27, 4:1 * 1 Timothy 3:8 * 2 Timothy 2:15 * Job 2:7 * 1 John 4:4 * Nahum 2:5 * Isaiah 43:1, 2, 3a * Daniel 3:26, 27 *

Ephesians 6:11, 13, 14 * Exodus 39:14 * Job 1:9-12, 2:6 * Psalm 91:11-13 * Hebrews 1:14 * 1 Kings 19:5 * Daniel 6:22 * Matthew 18:10 * John 6:44 * Isaiah 14:24, 46:10 * Jeremiah 1:5 * Genesis 18:12, 14 * Matthew 19:26 * Mark 10:27 * Luke 18:27 * Psalm 139:4

Chapter Fourteen: Exodus 25:7 * Exodus 28:9, 28:17-21 * Psalm 119:96 * Acts 8:39 * Matthew 17:20, 21, 21:21, 14:29 * Luke 17:6 * Habakkuk 2:14 * 1 John 4:1-3 * Daniel 12:9 * Psalm 34:7 * Acts 12:11 * Hebrews 13:2 * Matthew 13:35, 25:34 * Ephesians 1:3, 4 * Revelations 14:1-5 * Genesis 24:7, 40 * 1 Kings 19:5-8 * Daniel 6:22 * Acts 27:23, 24 * Revelation 7:1-4 * Ezekiel 37:15-22 * Isaiah 11:12 * James 1:1 * Isaiah 54:4-8 * Isaiah 11:1-9 * Revelation 5:5 * Genesis 48:1-20 * Revelation 7:6 * Matthew 24:36 * John 8:28 * Matthew 24:44 * Revelation 3:20 * Psalm 37:4 * Luke 19:24 * Ester 4:4 * Ruth 4:13-22 * Ruth 4:17 * Matthew 1:17 * Matthew 10:29 * Habakkuk 3:11 * Joshua 10:13 * Revelation 4:1-2 * Ephesians 6:12 * Genesis 2:7, 21, 22 * Revelation 12:7-9 * Isaiah 14:12-15 (KJV) * Ezekiel 28:13-17 * Luke 1:19 * Luke 2:10-12 * Matthew 1:20, 21 * Revelation 21:1-7 * Revelation 3:20

Chapter Fifteen: Hebrews 2:11

Chapter Eighteen: Jeremiah 50:6 * Luke 19:10 * 2 Corinthians 5:17 * Acts 2:28 * John 15:11, 16:24 * Matthew 5:14 * Ephesians 5:8 * Exodus 39:10-14

Chapter Nineteen: Romans 8:28 * Luke 23:44-46, 24:6-8 * Psalm 22 * Isaiah 53 * Matthew 16:24 * Mark 8:34 * Luke 9:23 * 1 Peter 1:2 * 1 John 4:4

Chapter Twenty One: Jeremiah 4:5, 6 * Joel 2:1 * Jeremiah 51:27 * Genesis 16:4a, 31 * 1 Samuel 17:4-50

Chapter Twenty Three: Revelation 9:16

Chapter Twenty Four: Revelation 9:15-18 * Daniel 7:4-7 * Revelation 17:3,12, 13 * 2 Chronicles 7:14 * Daniel 11:32b (KJV) * Matthew 24:6 * Jeremiah 6:14 * Revelation 7:4

Epilogue: Genesis 37:9 * Revelation 14:3 * Joel 2:32, 3:1, 2 * Ezekiel 37:15-22 * Revelation 14:1, 7:1-4, 12:17, 13:1, 2a, 5, 6, 20:10, 14: 9-11

A COVENANT

90% of the royalties from the sale of this novel will be used to purchase Bibles which will be distributed by Christian missionaries.

Printed in the United States
18214LVS00002B/100-339